THE PORTABLE FEAST

J.B. Pickett

THE PORTABLE FEAST

By Diane D. MacMillan
Drawings by Erni Young

101 Productions
San Francisco
1973

Distributed to the Book Trade in the United States of America
by Charles Scribner's Sons, New York

Distributed in Canada
by Van Nostrand Reinhold Ltd., Scarborough, Ontario

Library of Congress Catalog Card Number 72-94896

Second Printing, January, 1974

PUBLISHED BY 101 PRODUCTIONS
834 Mission Street
San Francisco, California 94103

Contents

The investigation of nature is an infinite pleasure-ground
where all may graze, and where the more bite,
the longer the grass grows,
the sweeter is its flavor and the more it nourishes.
—T. H. Huxley, 1871

Introduction

There are many kinds of portable feasts with a surprising number of variations from the elaborately planned picnic to the simple, impromptu affair. Impromptu picnics are often inspired by nature. They express man's need to return to a more natural environment. Through the centuries this impulse to explore unknown horizons, toting the meal, has been one of man's greatest pleasures. Today, the picnic is as much a part of the American tradition as the Fourth of July or apple pie. A meal shared with nature stimulates the appetite and amplifies the enjoyment of food.

A planned picnic can happen anytime at anyplace. It may be an event at the sports' stadium, a tour through the wine country, an afternoon out sailing, a day at the seashore, a bicycle excursion in the country or an outing on a leisurely Sunday.

The recipes in this book are very versatile and taste just as delicious indoors as they do outdoors. Should the weather cause problems, try a rainy-day picnic by a crackling fire. Picnic fare knows no season.

Vacation menus are also thought of as picnic fare. It is a time to cook simply, concentrating on easily but promptly prepared meals. Whatever the situation, it is a real challenge to transform an outdoor picnic into a gourmet meal.

Before embarking on an excursion, keep in mind the importance of food protection (see page 10) as well as a menu to complement the occasion. Make the menu picturesque and appetizing. Do not be confined to past menus and habits. An endless diet of fried chicken, tuna sandwiches and potato chips is hardly original. On the other hand, the silver candelabra and champagne glasses are not a prerequisite either. A picnic should stir up a feeling of anticipation for a simple, adaptable menu, reflecting your thought and effort.

For an adventure in good eating, I offer a versatile repast to fill your picnic hamper. I offer a means of pleasing the palate of outdoor companions by improving the quality of your portable feast. Whatever your traveling needs, whatever your destination, I assure you dining pleasures.

D.D.M.

Transporting the Fare

SAFETY DETAILS FOR FOOD PROTECTION AND TRANSPORTATION

When it comes to planning, details matter. It is no fun to arrive at your destination only to discover a major item missing such as a corkscrew. When the wanderlust impulse strikes you to pack a meal, play it safe. Pack with order, not at random.

The most important factor is menu selection. Avoid any disease-producing foods, high in protein and moisture (i.e., dairy products, eggs, poultry, fish, shellfish or foods containing mayonnaise such as sandwich fillings or potato salad), *unless* properly protected. Certainly sandwich fillings are safe if wrapped properly (see page 49) and kept in a cool place (not exceeding four to six hours) or in a cooler chest. For all-day traveling during warm weather these foods as well as creamed-filled pastries, creamed sauces and gravies are potentially hazardous due to bacteria. If you plan to tote them longer than the specified time or do not have the facilities to maintain the proper cool temperature, *do not take them.*

Bacteria also reacts to improperly handled or cooked foods. Protect food from contamination during and after preparation. Keep all foods covered, except when being prepared or served, and out of direct sunlight. Purchase perishables on the way, close to the time and place of eating. Preparing foods too far in advance reduces the quality and safety of a meal. Therefore, refrigeration is imperative for potentially hazardous foods.

Transporting food is a second important concern. The most common hampers come in wicker or plastic. For the best investment choose an enclosed, heavily insulated cooler chest. Foods can be kept cold on ice up to 48 hours or longer. Styrene-foam chests are inexpensive, lightweight and keep foods hot or cold for many hours.

Hot foods can be transported a short distance (two to four hours traveling time) in an insulated container. A hot casserole wrapped in foil and several thicknesses of newspaper retains heat for several hours. Insulated metal ice buckets will also keep things warm.

Cold foods must be refrigerated in a chest on plain ice or dry ice. Dry ice is packed on top of the food since the chilling gas (carbon dioxide) is heavier than air. Foods on ice are best protected placed in clean plastic containers.

Another method of refrigeration is the use of a container of frozen water, placed in the cooler chest at packing time. These containers can be purchased at hardware stores and supermarkets. For a makeshift container try a plastic distilled-water bottle, a clean milk carton or containers like Tupperware. Fill the container two-thirds full to allow for expansion during freezing. This method eliminates the problem of melted ice.

Thermosware is necessary for summer punch, hot soups or coffee braced with cognac for winter outings. For hot beverages heat the inside of the thermos with boiling water; for cold beverages chill with ice water. By keeping the container the same temperature as the liquid, it retains the desired temperature considerably longer.

Before leaving, make a list and check it. Always keep the picnic hamper ready, cleaned and replenished with supplies after each use. Then, your only concern the next departure will be meal preparation. Supply the hamper with a colorful plastic-coated material or terrycloth ground or table covering. Beach towels or roll-up reed mats make an excellent cover or the tailgate of a station wagon serves as a table. Cloth napkins, plastic or enamel plates and cups, and plastic glassware replace their soggy paper counterparts, eliminating excess refuse and ecology worries. Stock forks, knives, spoons, can opener, corkscrew, salt, pepper and your favorite condiments. An extra handy item is a small cheese or bread board for carving. Pack the items into the hamper in order of removal and use. Another convenience is a plastic bag with damp washcloths for any messy finger foods. Take along a water container, especially when traveling in remote areas. The water is also handy for clean-ups and a thirsty pet.

After eating, return all foods to the cooler chest. If there is no ice left or the slightest doubt that any food has been at an unsafe temperature, *throw it out*. The wisest plan is to manage the menu so that there are few or no leftovers.

Each of us who enjoys nature must take an interest in its preservation. Let's be *ecology-minded* with consideration for others who follow behind. At cleanup time if there are no trash cans, take all the remains, especially those that can be recycled, back home to be disposed of properly. Take along a container for all throwaways.

CHECK LIST

- *Hamper or Cooler Chest:* For cooler chest, freeze ice containers the night before.
- *Table or Ground Cover:* No-iron linen table-cloth, plastic-coated table cover, terry cloth beach towels or roll-up reed mats.
- *Napkins:* No-iron linen or terry cloth.
- *Cups or Glasses:* Insulated cups, plastic stack wine glasses.
- *Plates:* Plastic- or enamel-coated plates. Plastic plates come in square sizes and take up less space.
- *Flatware:* Forks, knives (one for carving), spoons and serving utensils.
- *Wine Bottle Opener:* Corkscrew.
- *Can Opener:* For beer or regular cans.
- *Condiments:* Salt, pepper, mustard, catsup and sugar.
- *Thermosware:* Regular one-quart size, short, individual wide-mouth containers, 1/2-gallon size.
- *Plastic Food Containers:* All sizes. Square containers that stack take up less packing space than round ones.
- *Hibachis, Bucket Broilers or Folding Grills:* For barbecue. Folding grills are made for picnic use at the beach or park and to fit over a campfire.
- *Charcoal*

Breads

Bread . . . strengthens man's heart,
and therefore called the staff of life.
—Matthew Henry: Exposition of Psalm CIV, 1705

HISTORY OF BREAD

Bread making is the foundation of many a traveling meal. In the beginning, man first ate seeds of grass. He learned to grind them into flour, mix them with water and bake them in either the sun or by fire. This gradually evolved into a bread of crushed acorns and beechnuts. Even today acorn cakes are eaten by Indians of the Pacific slopes. Among the 10,000-year-old remains of the Swiss Lake dwellers are signs of a baking industry. The Egyptian tombs tell the story of the bread ritual from planting to baking. In fact one 3,500-year-old loaf was actually found. During times of famine, bread was made with acorns, inner layers of pine bark, flour mixed with straw and even earth.

One of the earliest forms of bread is flat bread, thin wafers of unleavened baked dough. It is widely eaten in India, Iran and Armenia. Jewish bread, matzoth, is probably the best known of the flat breads. When the Israelites fled from the Egyptians, they did not have time to allow their bread to ferment. Today during Passover, their descendants eat unleavened bread in commemoration of this "bread of affliction."

The ancient Egyptians (some books say the Chinese) first discovered the technique of leavening bread with yeast or a similar type of fermentation. This art consists of allowing the dough to ferment long enough for gases to form a light loaf. The end product was a bread similar to what we know today, except it was not white but dark brown or black in color.

White flour is a fairly modern invention. Up until the last two centuries only nobility could afford white bread. (The peasants ate rye and barley bread and oatcakes.) Ironically much of the food value is removed during milling, bleaching, and processing. To compensate for this loss, white flours are enriched with vitamins and minerals. Wheat germ is one of the main ingredients which is removed. Whenever possible, add it to your baked goods unless you use whole-wheat flour. This enrichment is particularly important to people who depend on bread as the mainstay of their diets. In the United States, bread accounts for 20 percent of the total calories consumed while in other countries it is 50 percent or more.

Throughout the world bread is known by many names and made of many grains—wheat, corn, rye, barley, millet, oats and maize. Breads in America differ from breads of the Old World due to the use of sweetening, shortening, sometimes milk and eggs in addition to the basic *flour, water, leavening and salt.* In Scotland, the people enjoy oatcakes; in Germany, Russia and Scandinavia a common "black bread," rye sometimes with barley or potato flour added. In India, they break unleavened millet cakes and chapatties made from wheat. The Far Eastern countries prefer rice to breads. In Mexico and Latin America, they eat tortillas made from ground cornmeal. In Brazil people enjoy manioc flour cakes from the cassava root. And our pioneers going west and exploring Alaska brought with them the sourdough starter and bannock, flat loaves of unleavened bread.

Today's modern kitchens are so well equipped that it is not necessary to return to the methods of the Swiss Lake Dwellers or the ancient Egyptians to obtain an honest loaf of bread. Breads can be baked and frozen ahead of time. Other breads can be mixed, kneaded, shaped and frozen up to a month. When ready for use, defrost, allow to rise and bake. The new electric mixers with dough hooks simplify beating and mixing, help develop gluten and eliminate some of the time and effort involved in hand beating and kneading.

Baking and breaking bread with family and friends is an expression of love. It is a form of therapeutic involvement in a culture increasingly faced with computerized living. It is a rewarding culinary feat. Not only is there material satisfaction (which I might add won't last long) but a home filled with the aroma of freshly baked bread. And most important is the psychological satisfaction of preparing the historically essential staff of life. If you really know which side your bread is buttered on, you will bake your own bread.

YEAST

Yeast, the leavening agent in baking, is available in compressed yeast cakes or in the form of active dry granules. Compressed yeast is perishable and should be stored at 42° and may be frozen for up to three months. Once yeast is frozen and defrosted, it should not be refrozen. Active dry yeast needs no refrigeration. It comes in airtight, moistureproof packets which ensure freshness. One package of dry yeast equals one scant tablespoon (2¾ teaspoons) or one 0.6-ounce cake. Compressed or fresh yeast is available in 0.6-ounce cakes or 1-ounce and 2-ounce cakes. Either form of yeast can be used interchangeably in all recipes.

Remember yeast is a sensitive organism. Water or liquid hotter than 115° will kill the yeast and the bread will not rise. Between 105° to 115° is the best temperature for active dry yeast. The length of time it takes the dough to rise is proportional to the amount of yeast; the smaller the amount of yeast, the longer it will take the dough to rise. For best results, always follow the directions on the yeast package or recipe.

FLOUR

Since all types of flour vary greatly and are affected by humidity and handling, a person must acquire a "feel" for bread making to deal with those variances which influence the end result—your breads.

Flour has the capacity to absorb or lose moisture depending upon the humidity. This is the reason that flour in most recipes is given in fluctuating amounts (i.e. four to five cups). The amount and quality of gluten in flour also varies and is dependent upon the blending and kneading. Gluten is the substance that forms the structure of the loaf. Flours with a higher gluten content will yield breads with larger volume. Gluten allows bread to stretch and become elastic, holding the gas bubbles formed by the yeast. Gluten flour is available in health-food stores. An additional half cup can replace a half cup of unbleached flour in any bread recipe. Gluten bread is higher in protein and lower in starch than many other breads. Whole-wheat flour, which has less gluten than white flour produces a heavier, smaller loaf. Rice and soy flour, which have no gluten cannot be used alone to make yeast breads.

Never sift flour for bread making. Spoon it into the measuring cup, leveling with a spatula or straight-edged knife. Do not tap the cup or shake the flour down.

Kneading properly and leaving adequate time for the gluten to develop will result in a better loaf of bread. You can never under-knead, but you can work in too much flour. The correct consistency is reached when the dough adheres to itself. It will be smooth, nonsticky and spring back when pressed. When a recipe calls for four to eight cups of flour and the consistency seems correct after six cups of flour, do not work in the remaining amount. Each recipe includes full instructions, tips and techniques for that particular type of bread.

Keep whole-wheat flour, unbleached flour and wheat germ refrigerated to avoid rancidity. Allow them to reach room temperature before use or warm slightly in a slow oven in a shallow pan.

LIQUIDS

The usual liquids used in bread baking are milk, potato water or regular water. Unpasteurized milk should be scalded and cooled slightly. Water gives bread a crispy crust; milk gives bread a nutritious, soft crust; and potato water yields a larger, lighter loaf.

SALT

Salt stabilizes fermentation, controls the action of the yeast, slows the rising time and accents the flavor. Some people use more salt during the summer when heat speeds up fermentation.

SUGAR

From the standpoint of fermentation, sugar is not necessary in bread. However, it helps activate the yeast during the rising process. Not only does it add flavor but it improves texture and increases the browning potential of the crust. Try substituting brown sugar, honey or molasses for white sugar.

SHORTENING, FATS AND OILS

Butter, margarine or salad oils help the bread dough expand and stretch. They improve flavor, add richness, produce a fine texture and a tender moist loaf.

EGGS

Eggs are not essential in bread baking. However, they do provide nutrition, a delicate texture and additional flavor.

STORING BREAD

To keep homemade breads fresh and moist, wrap them in aluminum foil, plastic wrap or any airtight bag. Do not store them in the refrigerator or they will dry out. The one exception is an extremely warm, damp climate where refrigeration prevents molding.

Plan to use natural French or Italian breads within 24 to 48 hours. These breads lose their fresh flavor quickly and those without preservatives will mold and stale as will rye and pumpernickel. Freezing bread is another alternative.

SOURDOUGH STARTER

The sourdough starter is a fresh yeast culture used some 6,000 years ago by the Egyptians. The zesty aroma of American sourdough baking drifted across the western plains from the campfires of chuck wagons, homesteaders and prospectors. It gradually became known as "wilderness yeast."

Many prospectors carried their starter in flour sacks from which they prepared their sourdough flapjacks, biscuits and bannock. They would roll up leftover sourdough and place it in a scooped-out section of their flour supply. To keep the yeast warm and active on cold wintry nights, it was tucked in the bottom of the bedroll. Since yeast was often the most important single food (along with staples, sugar, salt, bacon and beans), the prospector took special care of it. If, on the other hand, he carried his starter in a crock, he enjoyed a few sips of the "beer" or "hooch" off the top. (After a starter sets, the solids sink to the bottom and a pungent liquid rises to the surface.) Through the years the popularity of sourdough among men of the west gave them the name "sourdoughs."

UNDERSTANDING AND MAINTAINING SOURDOUGH STARTER

The sourness of a starter depends upon how long and at what temperature it ferments. The warmer the spot, the more quickly it will ferment. For an effective sourdough starter, allow it to set 36 to 48 hours before using.

A starter can literally be kept forever if maintained properly. It should always be refrigerated; room temperature invites the growth of undesirable bacteria and molds. Yeast should be pungent, full of bubbles and increase in volume. Before using it, return one cup of starter back into the crockery container. Cover it with a tight-fitting, non-metal lid. It can be frozen and thawed and refrozen many times.

A starter should consist of *only* white flour, yeast, water or potato water and possibly a pinch of sugar now and then. Never add soda, eggs or baking powder; it will ruin the starter. And never add whole-wheat flour to the white flour-based starter. After several days in the refrigerator, the solids will sink to the bottom and a pungent odor will rise to the surface. Do not discard this liquid, called the sourdough "beer" or shades of "hooch." All that is necessary is to stir and blend it back together.

The night before baking, remove the starter from the refrigerator. Stir and blend it with equal parts water and flour. The standard amount is one cup of water to one cup of flour. Cover and put it in a draft-free spot. In the morning, pour out the needed amount, and return at least one cup to the refrigerator. Try to use the starter once a week.

Freshen the starter with equal amounts of flour and water or just a little flour as it sometimes thins out when not used too often. Freeze it if you do not intend to use it for several months. Always allow it to defrost and reactivate itself at room temperature for about 24 hours.

BASIC SOURDOUGH STARTER

1 package dry yeast
1 cup lukewarm water
1 cup unbleached white flour
pinch sugar

Combine yeast and lukewarm water. Stir until completely dissolved. Blend in the flour and sugar. Cover and allow to set in a warm draft-free spot in your kitchen for 2 days.

SOURDOUGH POTATO STARTER

1 medium potato
2-1/2 cups water
1 package dry yeast
2 teaspoons sugar
2 cups unbleached white flour

Peel and slice the potato. Boil in the water until tender. Drain and reserve 2 cups of the potato water. Cool to 115°. Blend in the yeast, sugar and approximately 2 cups of flour or enough to make a thick batter. Cover loosely and allow to set in a warm draft-free spot in your kitchen for 2 days. Potato starter and basic starter can be blended together.

WHOLE-WHEAT SOURDOUGH STARTER

1 package dry yeast
1/3 cup warm water
3/4 cup whole-wheat flour
additional 3-1/2 cups whole-wheat flour
2-1/2 to 3 cups warm water

Combine the yeast and warm water. Stir until completely dissolved. Blend in the 3/4 cup of flour and allow to set approximately 3 to 4 hours or until nice and bubbly, light and foamy. Now blend in the additional flour and warm water. Cover and allow to set in a draft-free spot for 24 to 48 hours. Whole-wheat starters must be kept separate from other types and used only for whole-wheat breads.

SOURDOUGH FRENCH BREAD

1 cup basic sourdough starter (prepared ahead)
1-1/2 cups warm water
1 package dry yeast
2 teaspoons sugar
2 teaspoons salt
4 cups white unbleached flour
1/2 teaspoon baking soda
additional 1-1/2 cups flour

The night before prepare your starter with equal amounts of flour and water (see page 18) 1 cup each, unless you intend to double the recipe. Pour out 1 cup of starter the next morning and set aside. Return the remainder of the starter back into the crock and refrigerate.

Pour the warm water into a large bowl. Sprinkle on the yeast and allow it to dissolve completely. Sprinkle on the sugar and salt; stir to blend. Add the 1 cup of starter. Gradually work in 4 cups of flour. Cover with a towel and set in a warm draft-free spot until the dough has doubled, approximately 1-1/2 to 2 hours. Turn out onto a well-floured surface or pastry cloth. Work in the combined baking soda and additional 1-1/2 cups flour. Knead, adding flour to control stickiness, until smooth and elastic. *Do not work in too much flour.* Knead 8 minutes. Place in a lightly greased bowl and turn once to coat evenly. Cover and allow to rise until double in bulk. Punch down and shape into 2 oblong loaves or 1 large round one. For 2 loaves, roll out each half into a 15x10-inch oblong shape and taper the ends. Place on a lightly greased baking sheet, cover and put in a warm place. Let it rise 1-1/2 to 2 hours, depending upon the room temperature. Place a shallow pan of water at the bottom of the oven. Preheat to 400°. Just before baking slash diagonally across the top of the loaves with a sharp, single-edged razor blade in 3 to 4 places. Brush loaves with cold water. Bake 40 to 45 minutes for oblong loaves, until crusty and brown or 55 minutes if one large round loaf. Remove and cool. For crackly crust, cool in a draft.

Better is half a loaf than no bread
—John Heywood: Proverbs 1546

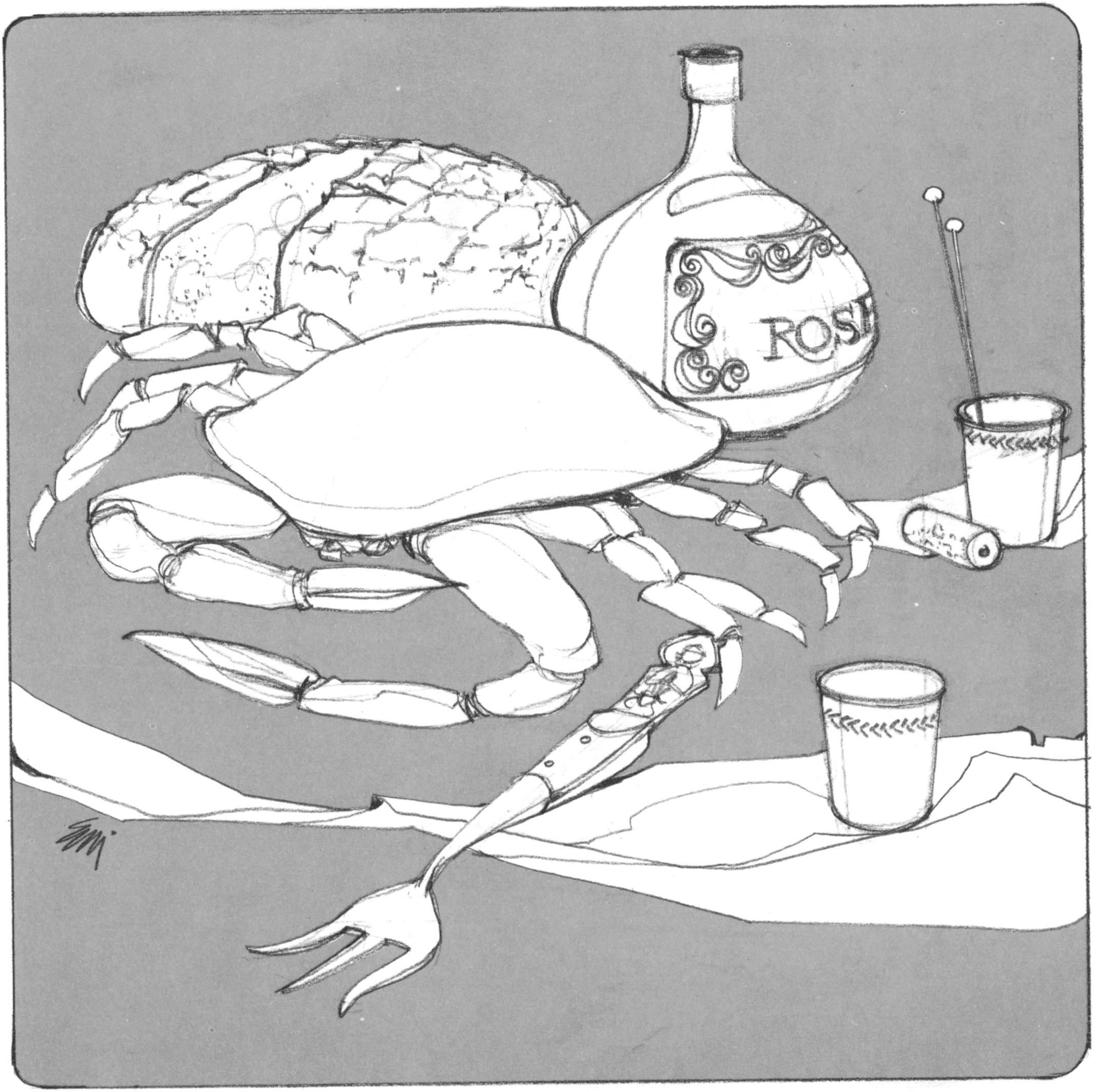
ROSE

SOURDOUGH HONEY-WHEAT BREAD

1 cup milk
1 package dry yeast
3 tablespoons butter
2 tablespoons honey
2 tablespoons molasses
2 cups basic or potato starter
2 to 2-1/2 cups white unbleached flour
1 cup whole-wheat flour
3 tablespoons wheat germ
1 teaspoon salt
1 tablespoon sugar
1 teaspoon baking soda
approximately 1 cup additional flour

Scald the milk, blending in the butter, honey and molasses; then set aside to cool. Pour into a bowl, sprinkle on the yeast and stir to dissolve. Add the 2 cups of starter. Combine the 2 cups of white flour, wheat flour and wheat germ together. Gradually work the blended flour into the milk mixture. Add salt, sugar and soda. Continue to blend until thoroughly combined. Cover and set in a draft-free warm place until doubled in size. Stir and punch down. Turn out onto a well-floured surface and knead working in additional white flour 1/2 cup at a time, until smooth and elastic (flour required will vary). Knead until satiny and smooth. Divide into 2 loaves and place them seam side down in 2 greased loaf pans. Brush tops with oil. Cover and set in a warm, draft-free place until doubled. Bake at 375° for 30 to 40 minutes or until the bread makes a hollow sound when tapped on the top. Remove, put on racks, brush tops with melted butter and allow to cool.
Makes 2 loaves

SOURDOUGH HERB BREAD

1 cup milk
3 tablespoons butter
1/4 cup sugar
1 package dry yeast
2 cups wheat or white starter
1/2 teaspoon crushed marjoram leaves
1/2 teaspoon crushed oregano leaves
1/2 teaspoon crushed basil leaves
pinch garlic powder (optional)
2 cups wheat flour
2 cups unbleached white flour
1/4 cup wheat germ
1-1/2 teaspoons salt
1 teaspoon baking soda

Scald the milk and melt the butter in it; then allow to cool. Pour into a large bowl and sprinkle in the sugar and yeast, stir until completely dissolved. Blend in the starter and herbs. Combine wheat flour and white flour, adding the wheat germ. Slowly add the flours to the milk mixture until the dough begins to pull away from the sides of the bowl. Cover and let rise until doubled in bulk. Turn out onto a well-floured surface and knead until smooth and elastic. Work in salt and baking soda. Punch down and divide into 2 loaves. Turn into 2 well-greased loaf pans. Brush tops with oil. Cover and let rise in a warm, draft-free place until doubled, approximately 1 hour. Bake at 375° for 35 to 40 minutes or until bread makes a hollow sound when tapped on the top. Remove from pans and cool on racks.
Makes 2 loaves

ITALIAN BREAD

2 teaspoons salt
1-1/2 teaspoons sugar
1 cup warm water
1 package dry yeast
3 cups flour
cornmeal
approximately 1 cup additional flour

The difference between Italian and French bread is that the French bread is crustier.

Stir salt and sugar into warm water in a large bowl. Sprinkle on the yeast. Cover until bubbly, approximately 5 to 8 minutes. Add the flour, gradually working it in 1 cup at a time. Beat at high speed 2 minutes, scraping the bowl occasionally. Add only enough additional flour to form a stiff dough. Turn into a greased bowl, turning dough over to coat evenly. Cover and let it rise 1-1/2 hours. Punch down, divide and shape into 2 loaves as in Sourdough French Bread (page 19).

Place loaves on a pan sprinkled with cornmeal and let rise 1 hour. Slash with a razor blade and brush with water as for French bread. Place in the middle of preheated 400° oven. Place a shallow pan of boiling water at the bottom of the oven. Bake for 45 to 50 minutes or until bread makes hollow sound when tapped on top.
Makes 2 loaves

ITALIAN WHOLE-WHEAT LOAF

2 cups warm water
2 packages dry yeast
1 tablespoon sugar
1 tablespoon salt
2 tablespoons softened butter
4-1/2 cups white unbleached flour
2 cups unsifted whole-wheat flour
cornmeal

Pour warm water into a bowl. Sprinkle on yeast and stir until dissolved. Blend in the sugar, salt and butter. Blend the flours then add them to the mixture; the dough will be very stiff. Turn out and knead until smooth and elastic. Place in a greased bowl and turn dough over to coat evenly. Cover and set in a draft-free, warm place until doubled in bulk, approximately 1-1/2 hours. Punch dough down, turn out onto a floured surface and knead. Divide in half; then roll and shape into 2 oblong loaves as for Sourdough French Bread (page 19). Lightly grease 2 baking sheets and sprinkle them with cornmeal. Place each loaf on a sheet, cover and allow to rise 1-1/2 hours. Slash with razor blade and brush with water. Place a shallow pan of hot water on the bottom of the oven. Bake the loaves at 375° 45 to 50 minutes or until the bread makes a hollow sound when tapped. Allow to cool on wire racks.
Makes 2 loaves

LIGHT-FLAVORED WHEAT BREAD

1 cup milk
1/4 pound butter
2 tablespoons sugar
1-1/2 teaspoons salt
1 package dry yeast
1/4 cup lukewarm water
1-1/2 cups unbleached white all-purpose flour, blended with 1/2 cup graham flour and 1/4 cup wheat germ
2 eggs, beaten
3 to 4 cups additional unbleached white flour

Scald the milk then add butter, sugar and salt to it. Set aside to cool slightly. In a large bowl dissolve yeast in lukewarm water. Blend in the combined flours and add just enough of the cooled milk mixture to form the consistency of cake batter. Cover and allow to set 20 minutes or until bubbly. Then beat in eggs and enough flour to form a stiff dough. Turn out onto a floured surface and knead until smooth and elastic, adding only enough flour to keep it from being sticky. Cover and allow to double for 1-1/2 hours. Punch down and divide into 2 equal portions. Shape and place in 2 greased bread pans. Cover and allow to rise and double once again, or until dough rises above the tops of the pans. Bake in preheated 375° oven for 30 minutes or until bread makes a hollow sound when tapped on the top. Brush with softened butter. Remove loaves from pans and cool.
Makes 2 loaves

WHITE BREAD

Use preceding recipe for wheat bread omitting combination flours and substituting unbleached flour.

YOGURT BREAD

1-1/2 cups whole-wheat flour
1 cup unbleached white flour
2 tablespoons wheat germ
2 teaspoons baking soda
1 teaspoon salt
1 pint unflavored yogurt, room temperature
1/2 cup molasses
1 cup currants
1/2 cup finely chopped walnuts or your choice

In a large bowl combine the flours, wheat germ, soda and salt. Blend in the yogurt, molasses, currants and chopped nuts. Mix thoroughly. Divide the batter evenly between 3 well-greased 1-pound coffee cans (or 3 8-1/2x4-1/2x2-inch loaf pans). Bake at 350° for 1 hour or until a toothpick inserted in the center comes out clean. Cool in the cans for 10 minutes; then turn out and stand upright on wire racks to cool. Wrap in airtight, plastic wrap or foil and keep refrigerated. Freezes well. Slice crosswise. Delicious served with cream cheese and marmalade.
Makes 3 small loaves

"Sans pain, sans vin, l'amour n'est rien!"
(Without bread, without wine, love is nothing)
—French proverb

BUTTERMILK OATMEAL BREAD

1-1/4 cups buttermilk
1 tablespoon sugar
2 teaspoons salt
3 tablespoons butter
1/2 cup oatmeal
1 package dry yeast
1/4 cup warm water
pinch of sugar
3 to 4 cups unbleached white flour
vegetable oil

Scald the buttermilk (it characteristically appears curdled and separated). Stir in sugar, salt, butter and oatmeal. Cool to lukewarm. Dissolve the yeast in warm water with a pinch of sugar and allow to set 5 minutes. Blend into the cooled milk mixture. Gradually work in 3 cups of flour, 1 cup at a time until it forms a stiff dough. Add additional flour only if necessary to control stickiness. Turn out onto a floured surface and knead, sprinkling lightly with flour to keep from getting sticky. Turn into a greased bowl, turning to coat evenly. Cover and allow to rise in a warm, draft-free place until doubled in bulk. Punch down, divide in half and shape into 2 loaves. Place each in a greased loaf pan and brush tops with oil. Cover and let rise until doubled. Bake at 375° for 35 to 40 minutes or until bread makes hollow sound when tapped on the top. Brush with melted butter and cool on wire racks.
Makes 2 loaves

COMBINATION, EXTRA-RICH LOAF

1 cup hot tap water
2 tablespoons dark molasses
3 tablespoons butter
1-1/4 teaspoons salt
1 package dry yeast
1 cup unbleached white flour
1/2 cup graham flour
1/4 cup wheat germ
1/2 cup cornmeal
approximately 1 cup additional flour

In a saucepan combine hot tap water, molasses and butter. Place over low heat until butter has completely melted. Set aside to cool slightly. In a large bowl combine the salt, flours, wheat germ, cornmeal and the dry yeast. Blend in the molasses mixture, adding just enough additional flour to form a stiff dough. Turn out onto a floured surface and knead until the dough is smooth and elastic and has lost all stickiness. Then turn dough over several times in a well-buttered clean bowl so that all sides are well greased. Cover and allow to double for 1-1/2 hours. Punch dough down, form into a loaf and place in a greased loaf pan. Cover and allow to double or until dough rises above the top of the pan. Bake at 375° for 30 to 35 minutes or until bread makes hollow sound when tapped on top. Remove from oven and turn out onto a cake rack to cool. The rich flavor of this bread goes well with cold cuts or cheese.
Makes 1 loaf

CHEDDAR CHEESE BREAD

6 to 7 cups unbleached white flour
1 tablespoon sugar
1 tablespoon salt
2 packages dry yeast
1-1/2 cups water
3/4 cup milk
3 cups shredded extra-sharp cheddar cheese
(approximately 3/4 pound)
1/4 teaspoon onion powder (optional)

In a large mixing bowl combine 3 cups of the flour, sugar, salt and the undissolved yeast. Combine water and milk in a saucepan and bring to just below boiling. Set aside to cool and then blend into the dry ingredients, beating and scraping the sides of the bowl occasionally. Add cheese and an additional 1/2 cup of flour which has been blended with the onion powder. Turn out onto a floured surface and knead until smooth and elastic, working in only enough flour to control stickiness. Place in a greased bowl, turning dough over to coat evenly. Cover and let rise in a warm, draft-free place until doubled in bulk. Punch down, turn out onto a floured surface and knead lightly. Cover and allow dough to rest 20 to 30 minutes. Punch down and divide in half. Shape into 2 loaves and place them in greased loaf pans. Cover and let rise until doubled in bulk, about 45 to 60 minutes. Bake at 375° 35 to 40 minutes or until bread makes hollow sound when tapped on top. Cool on wire racks.
Makes 2 loaves

RICOTTA CHEESE COUNTRY LOAF

1 package dry yeast
1/2 cup warm water
1/2 cup ricotta cheese (or well-drained
creamed cottage cheese)
2 tablespoons butter
1 egg, beaten
1/2 cup finely minced onion
1 tablespoon sugar
1 tablespoon caraway seeds
1 tablespoon salt
1 teaspoon baking soda
1/2 cup wheat germ
2 to 3 cups unbleached white flour

Dissolve yeast in warm water. In a saucepan combine the ricotta cheese with butter and heat until the butter melts. In a bowl combine the egg, onion, sugar, caraway, salt and baking soda and blend thoroughly. Blend in ricotta cheese mixture then add the dissolved yeast. Gradually blend in the wheat germ and flour until it forms a stiff dough. Cover and let rise in a warm, draft-free place until doubled in bulk. Punch down. Turn out onto a floured surface and knead until smooth and elastic, lightly dusting with flour to control stickiness. Pat and press into a 9-inch round cake pan at least 2 inches deep or a casserole. Cover and let rise until doubled in bulk. Bake at 350° for 40 minutes or until bread makes hollow sound when tapped on the top. Cool on wire rack.
Makes 1 loaf

DARK GERMAN RYE BREAD

3 cups unbleached white flour
3-1/2 cups rye flour
2 cups milk
1 tablespoon salt
1/3 cup dark molasses
3 tablespoons grated orange rind
1 tablespoon caraway seeds
4 tablespoons butter
1-1/2 cups ale
2 packages dry yeast
vegetable oil

Combine the white and rye flours together and set aside. Scald the milk; stir in the salt, molasses, grated orange rind, caraway seeds and butter. Set aside to cool. Heat the ale until warm, but not hot (105° to 115°) and pour it into a large mixing bowl; sprinkle on the yeast, stir until dissolved and add the lukewarm milk mixture. Gradually work in 3-1/2 cups of the blended flours beating until smooth. Cover this batter and set aside in a warm, draft-free place until doubled in bulk. Stir batter down and beat in just enough additional flour to form a stiff dough. Turn out onto a floured surface and knead until elastic and smooth, adding the blended flour, but again only enough to control the stickiness. Place in a greased bowl, turning to coat evenly. Cover, set in a warm place and allow to rise until doubled in bulk. Punch down and divide in half. Shape each half into a round loaf; place on a well-greased baking sheet or in 2 greased 8-inch pie plates. Brush the tops with oil. Slash tops of loaves with a razor or very sharp knife. Cover and let rise until doubled. Bake at 375° for 35 to 40 minutes or until bread makes a hollow sound when tapped on top. Cool on wire racks.
Makes 2 loaves

BAUERNBROT
(Viennese Rye)

3 cups white unbleached flour
2 cups rye flour
1 cup warm water
1 package dry yeast
1-1/2 cups white or wheat starter
1 tablespoon salt
1 tablespoon caraway seeds
3 tablespoons softened butter
1 teaspoon cornstarch
1/2 cup cold water
coarse salt (optional)
approximately 1 cup additional white flour

Combine white and rye flours together. Pour warm water into a bowl; sprinkle on the dry yeast and stir until completely dissolved. Blend in the starter, salt, caraway seeds and the soft butter. Beat in 2 cups of the flour, beating until smooth. Then gradually work in just enough flour to form a stiff dough. Add additional white flour only if necessary to obtain the proper consistency. Turn out onto a floured surface and knead until smooth and elastic. Add a dusting of flour to your hands to avoid stickiness. Turn dough into a greased bowl, turning dough over to coat evenly. Cover and let rise in a warm, draft-free place until doubled in bulk. Punch down and divide dough in half. Shape into 2 round loaves and place on greased baking sheets. Cover and allow to rise in a warm place until doubled in bulk. Bake at 350° for 35 to 40 minutes or until bread makes hollow sound when tapped. Just before bread is done, combine the cornstarch and cold water in a saucepan, and bring it to a boil then cool slightly. When the bread is baked, brush it with the cornstarch mixture and return to the oven for 3 minutes. Remove to wire racks to cool. If desired, sprinkle tops lightly with coarse salt on the cornstarch glaze just after baking. Makes 2 loaves

BOHEMIAN BREAD

2 packages dry yeast
1 cup unbleached white flour
1-1/2 cups whole-wheat flour
1/2 cup rye flour
1/4 cup wheat germ
2 cups milk
1/2 cup brown sugar
2 tablespoons molasses
4 tablespoons butter
1 tablespoon salt
2-1/4 to 2-1/2 cups additional white flour

Combine the dry yeast with the flours and wheat germ in a large mixing bowl. Heat the milk, brown sugar, molasses, butter and salt together, stirring until the butter melts. Allow to cool and then add to the dry mixture. Beat until smooth, scraping bowl occasionally. Gradually work in 2-1/4 to 2-1/2 cups additional white flour, but only enough to form a moderately stiff dough. Turn out onto a floured surface and knead until smooth and elastic. Place in a greased bowl, turning over to coat evenly. Cover and let dough double, approximately 1-1/2 hours. Punch down, divide in half and shape into 2 loaves. Place in 2 greased loaf pans, cover and allow dough to rise once again until doubled, about 1 hour. Bake at 375° for 40 minutes, or until bread makes a hollow sound when tapped on the top. Brush with melted butter and cool on wire racks.
Makes 2 loaves

PEANUT BUTTER BREAD

1/2 cup peanut butter, creamy or chunk-style
4 tablespoons butter
2 cups unbleached white flour
2-1/2 teaspoons baking powder
3/4 teaspoon salt
1/2 cup sugar
2 teaspoons grated orange rind (optional)
1/2 cup currants
1 egg, slightly beaten
1 cup milk

Prepare a day ahead and wrap in foil; this loaf slices best after it has set 24 hours.

Cream peanut butter and butter together until light and fluffy. Sift flour, baking powder and salt together and mix in the sugar. Add to the peanut butter mixture and blend with a spoon or fork, until it forms fine crumbs. Add grated orange rind and currants. Beat egg and milk together. Blend into the flour mixture and stir until just well moistened. Turn into a greased loaf pan. Bake at 350° for 55 to 60 minutes or until a toothpick inserted in the center comes out clean. Cool bread in the pan 10 minutes before turning out on a wire rack to cool completely. Serve with jam.
Makes 1 loaf

HERB-SEASONED PICNIC LOAF

1 package dry yeast
1/4 cup warm water
1 tablespoon sugar
1/4 teaspoon crushed sweet basil
1/4 teaspoon crushed oregano
1-1/2 cups buttermilk
3 tablespoons olive oil
2 teaspoons salt
4-1/2 cups *sifted* unbleached white flour
1/2 cup grated Parmesan cheese

Dissolve yeast in warm water. Set aside for 5 minutes or until bubbly. Stir in sugar, sweet basil and oregano. Heat buttermilk to lukewarm. Blend into the yeast mixture along with the olive oil and salt. Gradually add flour 1 cup at a time until it forms a stiff dough. Work in the grated Parmesan cheese. Turn into a well-greased 2-quart casserole. Brush with olive oil; cover and allow to rise in a warm, draft-free place until doubled in bulk, approximately 1 to 1-1/2 hours. Bake at 350° for 55 to 60 minutes or until bread makes hollow sound when tapped on top. Cool on wire racks.
Makes 1 loaf

BACON BREAD

1/2 pound (or 12 slices) of bacon
2 cups unbleached white flour
1/3 cup sugar
1 tablespoon baking powder
1 teaspoon salt
1/2 teaspoon baking soda
2 eggs, beaten
1/2 pint sour cream
1/3 cup milk

Cut bacon slices into very small pieces. Fry until crisp and then drain in a sieve, shaking now and then. Turn out onto paper towels to cool. Sift the flour, sugar, baking powder, salt and baking soda together. Combine the eggs, sour cream and milk, beating until well blended. Add this to the dry ingredients all at once and stir with a wooden spoon just enough to moisten. Fold in the bacon bits. Turn batter into a well-greased and floured 8-1/2x4-1/2-inch loaf pan. Bake at 350° for 50 to 55 minutes or until a toothpick inserted in the center comes out clean. Allow to cool in the pan about 10 to 15 minutes. Turn out onto a wire rack to cool completely.
Makes 1 loaf

Nature goes her own way, and all that to us seems an exception is really according to order.
—J. W. Goethe: 1824

ARMENIAN "PEDA" BREAD

1 package dry yeast
1/4 cup warm water
3/4 cup milk
1 tablespoon sugar
1/2 teaspoon salt
1-1/2 tablespoons olive oil
3 cups unbleached white flour
olive oil
1 egg yolk, mixed with 1 tablespoon water
sesame seeds

In a large bowl dissolve the yeast in warm water and stir to blend. In a saucepan heat the milk with the sugar, salt and olive oil. Allow to cool then stir into the dissolved yeast. Beat in 1-1/2 cups of flour; then gradually beat in enough additional flour to form a stiff dough. Turn out onto a floured surface and knead for 5 minutes or until smooth and elastic. Try not to work in too much additional flour or bread will be too heavy. Cover with a towel and let dough rest for 30 minutes. Punch down and knead once again. Pinch off a small portion of dough, about 1/4 cup in size, and form a small ball; make a big ball out of the larger portion. Flatten and pat the *large* one into a round cake about 1 inch thick. Poke a hole through the center and with your hands pull and stretch the dough in opposite directions to make a large doughnut-shaped loaf. Place on a greased baking sheet. Flatten and press the *small* ball into the center hole of the larger loaf. Brush with olive oil. Cover with plastic wrap and refrigerate 8 to 24 hours. Remove 30 minutes before baking time and allow to rise a bit more. Brush with the beaten egg-water mixture and sprinkle generously with the sesame seeds. Bake at 350° for 25 to 35 minutes, being sure that the bread does not overbrown. It should be golden and make a hollow sound when tapped on the top.
Makes 1 loaf

ARAB (SYRIAN) PITA BREAD

3 to 5 cups unbleached white flour
1-1/2 teaspoons sugar
2 teaspoons salt
2 packages dry yeast
2-1/2 cups very warm water
3 tablespoons olive oil
approximately 1 cup additional flour

In a large bowl combine 2 cups of the flour, sugar, salt and undissolved yeast. Gradually add the warm water to the dry ingredients and beat with a wooden spoon (or a heavy-duty electric mixer) until completely moistened. Add the oil and 3/4 cup more flour, beating at high speed and scraping the bowl occasionally. Add only enough additional flour to form a soft dough. Turn out onto a floured surface and knead 8 to 10 minutes until smooth and elastic. Place in a greased bowl in a warm, draft-free place until doubled in bulk, about 1 hour. Punch dough down, turn out onto a floured surface, cover and allow to rest 30 minutes. Roll into a 16-inch long log, then cut into 16 equal pieces. Roll each piece into a small ball then flatten each ball with a rolling pin into a 6-1/2-inch circle approximately 3/16-inch thick. Place on a lightly floured surface and let stand at room temperature uncovered for 1 hour. Do not place the dough where it is warm and might rush the rising process. There are two methods of baking these pitas. Choose the most convenient for you.

#1 Preheat the oven to 450°. Put each circle of bread on the "floor" of the oven. (Cover bottom of oven with foil ahead of time, if desired.) Bake 4 at a time for 5 minutes or until done. To brown the tops, put them under a hot broiler 3 inches from the heating unit for 1 minute or less, watching carefully.

#2 Cut out 16 7-inch squares of foil. Place each flattened circle of dough on a square of foil and set aside to rise uncovered for 1 hour. Move oven rack to the lowest position and preheat oven to 500°. Place 4 pitas at a time in the oven with the foil placed directly on the lowest rack. Bake 5 minutes or until puffed and lightly tanned.

After removing the pitas from the oven place them in a plastic bag or cover with a cloth while cooling to keep them pliable and moist. When cool freeze them for another time, then simply defrost them in the bag. To reheat place several wrapped in foil in a 400° oven or among the coals of a campfire for 10 to 15 minutes. Another method is to remove foil and place each frozen pita directly on the lowest rack for just 5 minutes or until heated.

In the Middle East people tear these breads into chunks and use them to scoop up their food (see recipe on page 122). By slitting them open on one side you can make a pocket for all sorts of interesting fillings.

Makes 16 pitas

FREEZE NOW—BAKE IT LATER BRIOCHE BRAID

1 cup unbleached white flour
1/2 cup sugar
1/2 teaspoon salt
2 packages dry yeast
1/2 cup milk
6 tablespoons butter
1/2 cup warm water
4 eggs, room temperature
2 teaspoons grated lemon peel
3-1/2 to 4 cups additional flour
1 egg white
1 tablespoon sugar

In a large mixing bowl combine the flour, sugar, salt and yeast. Scald the milk. Add the butter to the hot milk, stir until melted and blend in the warm water. Set aside to cool to 115°; then gradually stir into the dry ingredients, beating for 2 to 3 minutes, scraping sides of the bowl occasionally. Blend in the eggs and lemon peel, and beat an additional 2 to 3 minutes. Add additional flour, 1 cup at a time and *only* enough to form a soft dough. Turn out onto a well-floured surface and knead lightly until smooth and elastic. Cover with a towel and allow dough to rest 30 to 40 minutes. Punch down and divide dough in half. Divide each half into 3 equal pieces. Using palms of your hands, roll each piece into a 12-inch long strip. Braid 3 strips and pinch ends together to seal. Repeat with remaining 3 strips. Place each braid on a greased baking sheet. Cover tightly with plastic wrap and freeze until firm. Transfer to plastic bags. Can keep frozen 1 month. Remove from freezer, unwrap and place on ungreased baking sheets. Lightly cover and allow to stand at room temperature until completely thawed, about 3 to 4 hours. Let bread rise in warm, draft-free place until doubled in bulk, approximately 1-1/2 to 2 hours. Combine egg white and sugar. Brush mixture on breads. Bake at 350° for 25 to 30 minutes or until bread makes a hollow sound when tapped on top. Cool on wire racks.
Makes 2 braids

BAGELS

1-1/2 cups unbleached white flour
3 tablespoons sugar
1 tablespoon salt
1 package dry yeast
1-1/2 cups very warm water
3-1/2 to 4 cups additional flour
1 egg white mixed with
  1 tablespoon cold water

Combine the 1-1/2 cups flour, sugar, salt and undissolved yeast in a large mixing bowl. Blend in the warm water and beat for a few minutes. Gradually work in 1/2 cup of the additional flour, beating again and scraping the bowl occasionally. Add just enough flour to form a stiff dough. Turn out onto a floured surface and knead until smooth and elastic. Place in an *un*greased bowl. Cover and let rise in a warm, draft-free place for just 20 minutes; do not allow this dough to double in bulk.

Punch down and knead lightly on a floured surface. Roll into a 12x10-inch rectangle, then cut dough into 12 equal strips, each 1 by 10 inches. Form into doughnut-shaped rings, pinching ends of the strips together firmly to form a circle. Place on *un*greased baking sheets, cover and let rise in a warm place for another 20 minutes; do not allow dough to double.

In a 12-inch skillet bring 2 inches of water to a boil, then lower heat and simmer. Gently add a couple of bagels at a time to the water and simmer approximately 7 minutes. Remove to a towel to drain and cool. Bake on *un*greased baking sheets at 375° for 10 minutes. Remove from the oven and glaze with beaten egg white and cold water. Return them to the oven and bake additional 20 minutes. Cool on wire racks. Bagels can be frozen and reheated. Serve with cream cheese and smoked salmon or split and toasted.

Makes 12 bagels

Wes Brot ich ess, des Lied ich sing,
Whose bread I eat, his song I sing.
—Anonymous German saying

BOLILLOS
(Mexican oval-pointed rolls, like French bread)

2 cups water
1 tablespoon sugar
1-1/2 teaspoons salt
2 tablespoons butter
1 package dry yeast
4-1/2 to 5 cups unbleached white flour
1 teaspoon cornstarch
1/2 cup water

In a saucepan heat the water with the sugar, salt and butter until the butter completely melts. Set aside to cool slightly. Combine the cooled mixture and yeast in a bowl and stir until yeast dissolves. Gradually work in the flour, 1 cup at a time until it forms a stiff dough. Turn out onto a floured surface and knead, adding additional flour only to control stickiness. Place in a greased bowl, cover and let rise in a warm, draft-free place until doubled in bulk, about 1-1/2 hours. Punch down and turn out onto floured surface. Knead lightly to remove any air bubbles. Break off dough into 16 equal portions and shape into rolls. Slightly taper each roll at the ends as you would for French bread. Place on greased baking sheets a few inches apart. Cover and let rise 35 to 45 minutes or until doubled in size. In a small saucepan blend the cornstarch and the water. Bring just to a boil, remove from the heat and cool slightly. Brush glaze on each roll. With a razor blade make a 2-inch slash lengthwise along the top of each roll. Bake at 375° 35 to 40 minutes or until nicely browned. Cool on wire racks.
Makes 16 rolls

BURGER BUNS

2 cups unbleached white flour
1/4 cup dry milk
3 tablespoons sugar
3 teaspoons salt
2 packages dry yeast
3 tablespoons butter
2 cups very warm tap water
3/4 to 1 cup additional flour

In a large mixing bowl combine the flour, dry milk, sugar, salt and the undissolved dry yeast. Melt butter and set aside. Gradually add the warm water to the flour mixture and beat, scraping the sides of the bowl occasionally. Blend in the cooled melted butter. Work in 3/4 cup to 1 cup of additional flour, but only enough to form a stiff dough. Turn out onto a floured surface and knead 8 to 10 minutes, dusting with flour, but again only adding enough flour to control stickiness. Form into a ball and place in a greased bowl, turning over to grease evenly. Cover and place in a warm, draft-free place until doubled in bulk. Punch down and allow to rise one more time, approximately 30 minutes. Divide dough in half, then each half into approximately 8 to 10 pieces, depending upon how large a bun you desire. Form each piece into a ball. Place on greased baking sheets a few inches apart and press each bun slightly to flatten. Cover with a towel and once again place in a warm, draft-free place to rise and double a third time, approximately 50 to 60 minutes. Bake at 375° for 15 to 20 minutes. Cool on wire racks.
Makes 16 to 20 buns

CARDAMOM BUNS

1-1/2 cups milk
1/4 pound butter
1/2 cup sugar
1/2 cup warm water
1 package dry yeast
1-1/2 teaspoons powdered cardamom
2 eggs, room temperature, beaten
1 teaspoon salt
4 to 5 cups unbleached white flour
1 egg white, slightly beaten
1/4 cup finely ground almonds
granulated sugar

Scald the milk and remove from heat. Stir in the butter and sugar until butter has melted and the sugar has dissolved. Set aside to cool. In a separate bowl pour the warm water. Sprinkle on the yeast and stir until completely dissolved. Cover and let this mixture set for 5 minutes. In a large mixing bowl blend the slightly cooled milk mixture, dissolved yeast, powdered cardamom, beaten eggs and salt. Gradually work in the flour, one cup at a time until it forms a stiff dough. Turn out onto a floured surface and knead until smooth and elastic, adding only enough flour to control the stickiness. Place in a greased bowl, cover and set in a warm draft-free place to rise and double in size. Punch down and divide dough in half. Generously butter 2 9- or 10-inch square baking pans. Pull dough apart into equal size portions, and form into approximately 18 to 20 rolls. Arrange the rolls side by side in the pans. Brush with melted butter. Cover and set in a warm draft-free place to rise and double in bulk, about 45 minutes. Brush tops with beaten egg white, sprinkle with ground almonds and then lightly with sugar. Bake at 375° 25 to 30 minutes. Remove from pans and cool on wire racks. These can be frozen and reheated.
Makes 18 to 20 rolls

PIZZA DOUGH

1 cup warm water
1 package dry yeast
2 teaspoons sugar
2 teaspoons salt
2 tablespoons olive oil
2-1/2 to 3-1/4 cups unbleached white flour

Pour warm water into a large bowl and sprinkle on the yeast stirring until completely dissolved. Blend in sugar, salt, olive oil, and 1-1/2 cups of the flour. Beat until smooth, gradually adding more flour until it forms a stiff dough. Turn out onto a well-floured surface and knead 8 to 10 minutes until smooth and elastic, adding only enough flour to control the stickiness. Place in a greased bowl, cover and allow to rise in a warm, draft-free place for 1 hour.

Punch dough down, divide in half. Roll and stretch each portion into a 12-inch round—pizza pan or on a cookie sheet—or press into a 9x13-inch pan. Press dough up around the edges to form a rim of the dough. Bake at 350° for 8 to 10 minutes.

If desired, cool your pizza, then wrap it tightly in foil or plastic and store it in the refrigerator for several days before using. When ready to bake, unwrap pizza and place it on an ungreased baking sheet or pizza pan. Cover it with sauce and topping and bake at 450° for 20 to 25 minutes, or until the filling is bubbly and the crust is crisp.
Makes 2 pizza crusts

GINGER BISCUITS

2 cups unbleached white flour
1/2 teaspoon salt
4 teaspoons baking powder
1/2 teaspoon baking soda
1/4 cup sugar
5 tablespoons butter or shortening
1/2 cup minced crystallized ginger
1 cup buttermilk
melted butter or salad oil

Sift flour, salt, baking powder, soda and sugar together. Cut in the butter or shortening and blend until the mixture resembles coarse crumbs. Stir in the minced ginger. Add the buttermilk all at once and stir until the dough follows the spoon around the bowl. Turn out on a lightly floured surface and knead 1 minute. Roll 3/8 inch thick; brush with melted butter or salad oil; fold over and cut with a biscuit cutter. Bake on an ungreased cookie sheet in a preheated 450° oven 12 to 15 minutes.
Makes 24 small biscuits

Toting Box and Pail

Sandwiches
Thermos Treats and Desserts

*In the woods a man casts off his years,
as the snake his slough, and at what period
soever of life, is always a child.
—R. W. Emerson: Nature, 1836*

SANDWICHES

The earliest mention of the sandwich dates back to the Romans. They called it *ofela* which means snack. The Scandinavians also popularized the Danish open-face sandwich in the name of smørrebrød. But the sandwich that made history consisted of layered roast beef between two slices of bread. The fourth Earl of Sandwich, John Montagu, was a notorious 18th century gambler. Rather than take time from his pleasures to eat, he would order "a sandwich" as a simple matter of convenience.

The legend behind the famous hero or poor boy sandwich originated in France. The French word "pourboire" means tip or the same as a dime for a cup of coffee, a beggar's cry. The poor boys would knock on the doors of the convents crying "pourboire." Rather than let them go hungry, the nuns would scrape out the larder, assembling left-overs between French bread. Today many of us assemble our sandwiches in the tradition of the "poor boy" or "Dagwood," creating unusual sandwiches out of leftovers.

When packing the lunch box, do so with imagination. Millions of people take meals to work and to school and look forward to more than a peanut butter sandwich. During the winter months encourage hot foods such as soup, chili or stew, using one of the many wide-mouth thermoses. And don't forget the extras: cheeses, deviled eggs, salads, relishes and finger foods. Whatever the meal, consider mineral and vitamin requirements.

THE BREAD

My main conviction is that a truly perfect sandwich starts with fresh, homemade bread. Whenever possible, leave on the crust; it is full of vitamins and prevents sandwiches from drying out. For hearty sandwiches slice homemade breads 1/2-inch thick.

To avoid soggy sandwiches on picnics take along the ingredients separately in the cooler chest and assemble them just before eating. This is also an excellent way to make a festive smørrebrød party, offering a variety of foods to choose from. As you can see, sandwich building is quite an art and an epicure's delight.

THE SPREAD

When using butter, keep it at room temperature for easier spreading. Cover the bread to the edge of the crust. This will prevent fillings from soaking into breads. Cream cheese or peanut butter also prevent soggy sandwiches.

Remember when spreads or fillings include mayonnaise or cream cheese, prepared in the morning, they are safe until about midday unless refrigerated.

FILLINGS

Be sure fillings are moist, not wet. Store fillings in airtight containers in the refrigerator and when transporting them in a cooler chest. Try watercress in place of lettuce on sandwiches or, at least, vary the kinds of lettuce used. Spinach leaves, shredded cabbage, alfalfa sprouts, thin slices of cucumber or sliced radishes.

WRAPPING

Avoid sandwiches that dry out or leak liquids. Wrap everything securely and, whenever possible, in plastic, take-home containers. Using a box and pail instead of a brown bag is a step toward better ecology. Avoid the use or overuse of paper, plastic wrap and foil products as they are nonbiodegradable. The lunch box and pail as well as plastic food containers are highly recommended. They do away with litter, are easy to keep clean, carry a wide variety of foods, provide durable, economical service and eliminate the continual purchase of paper wrap. You need not feel guilty about cheating the garbage can. However, if you still insist on brown bagging your lunch, use bags of recycled paper. Every effort helps our environment.

For sandwiches, use waxed paper or parchment paper. You can purchase plastic containers made especially for sandwiches. If you prepare sandwiches ahead, store them in the refrigerator. Do not hold them longer than six hours. For picnics label each sandwich to avoid unwrapping them.

FREEZING SANDWICHES

Sandwiches without mayonnaise or lettuce can be frozen ready for that planned or impromptu picnic. Spread bread with softened butter all the way to the edge of the crust before filling. Wrap tightly and seal with freezer tape. Label and place sandwiches in a plastic bag and freeze. Frozen sandwiches are simply dropped into the lunch box in the morning and will be thawed by noon. Freezing a sandwich keeps it cold and fresh longer.

COMPLEMENTARY SANDWICH COMBINATIONS

The art of the sandwich is built layer upon layer, bite upon bite. The deeper the bite, the better the sandwich should be. This, of course, depends upon the combination and choice of ingredients. A good sandwich from the delicatessen or kitchen might consist of the following complementary sandwich combinations. Begin with homemade bread.

Cream cheese blended with Italian pesto sauce, sliced tomatoes and cucumbers
Cream cheese (or cottage cheese), cucumber slices and watercress
Cream cheese, chopped almonds and alfalfa sprouts
Cream cheese and marmalade, raisins and chopped nuts
Cream cheese, canned cranberry jelly and lettuce or watercress

Cream cheese blended with chopped olive, chopped nuts and fresh spinach leaves
Cream cheese with grated orange rind and chopped pecans
Cream cheese (or cottage cheese) with sliced avocado, sunflower seeds and alfalfa sprouts
Deviled egg, shredded cheddar cheese, minced green onions and fresh spinach leaves
Deviled egg, thin slices cucumber and fresh spinach leaves or alfalfa sprouts
Deviled egg, blended with crisp bacon bits, tomato slices and lettuce
Deviled egg, tuna, sliced tomatoes and alfalfa sprouts or watercress
Shrimp, avocado, minced green onions and alfalfa sprouts
Avocado, bean sprouts, tomato and lettuce
Avocado, shredded cheddar, chopped green onions and shredded lettuce
Turkey, cranberry jelly, chopped nuts and lettuce
Ham and thin layer of chutney
Ham and turkey, sliced hard-boiled egg, tomato, cheese and lettuce
Tuna and olive, thin cucumber slices, pimiento strips and lettuce
Tuna mixed with chopped nuts and fresh spinach leaves
Sardines, sliced hard-boiled egg, tomato, cucumber and alfalfa sprouts
Peanut butter, sliced bananas and chutney
Peanut butter, well-drained crushed pineapple and sliced banana
Peanut butter, grated carrot and raisins
Peanut butter and sliced peaches
Peanut butter, chopped dates and orange marmalade
Peanut butter, applesauce and raisins
Sliced chicken or turkey with bacon, tomato and fresh spinach leaves
Sliced chicken or turkey, paper-thin slices onion and lettuce
Chicken salad with chopped almonds, lettuce or watercress and tomato
Turkey, avocado and alfalfa sprouts
Corned beef, onion slices and well-drained coleslaw
Sliced broiled chicken livers, bacon, thin slices onion, tomato and lettuce
Liverwurst, broiled bacon and tomato, lettuce and thin slices cucumber
Sliced raw mushrooms, bacon and fresh spinach leaves
Sliced raw mushrooms, sliced raw zucchini, tomato and chopped green onions
Tomato, thin slices raw zucchini and alfalfa sprouts
Tomato, marinated artichoke hearts, lettuce
Tomato, broiled bacon and cheddar cheese, lettuce or fresh spinach leaves
Feta cheese, sliced olives, sliced tomato and alfalfa sprouts or fresh spinach leaves
Shredded cabbage, shredded carrot, chopped green onions and bean sprouts; bind with mayonnaise
Sliced hearts of palm, tomato and watercress
Ricotta cheese, tomato, chopped green onions and lettuce
Sliced cold, leftover sweetbreads, thin layer of mayonnaise, tomato and lettuce

POURBOIRE
(Poor Boy Sandwich)

1 loaf sourdough French bread
mayonnaise or softened butter
1 large tomato, sliced paper thin
crushed tarragon
2 hard-boiled eggs, sliced
1 medium cucumber, peeled,
  sliced paper thin
salt and freshly ground pepper
1 sweet red onion, sliced paper thin
3 to 4 ounces thinly sliced salami
3 to 4 ounces thinly sliced Gruyère or
  Swiss cheese
3 to 4 ounces smoked ham, sliced paper thin

Slice loaf in half lengthwise, spread with mayonnaise if desired or a thin layer of softened butter. Layer with thin slices of tomato and sprinkle with crushed tarragon. Next layer with eggs, cucumber and sprinkle with salt and freshly ground black pepper. Spread with thin slices of onion, salami and cheese. Start at the beginning and repeat the layers one more time. Place top of the bread over the layered filling and enjoy.
Serves 4 to 6

ITALIAN HERO

1 loaf Italian bread (page 24) or
  Italian whole-wheat loaf (page 24)
mayonnaise
1 large tomato, sliced paper thin
olive oil
crushed dry or minced fresh sweet basil
1 medium cucumber or
  raw zucchini, sliced paper thin
salt and freshly ground black pepper
1 sweet red onion, sliced paper thin
4 ounces Provolone cheese, thinly sliced
4 ounces Genoa salami, thinly sliced
1 green pepper, sliced in paper-thin rings,
  seeds removed
minced pickled pepperoni (Italian chili peppers)

Slice loaf in half lengthwise and spread with thin amount of mayonnaise, if desired. Layer with thin slices of tomato and sprinkle lightly with olive oil and sweet basil. Next layer with cucumber or zucchini and sprinkle with salt and pepper. Then layer with onion, cheese, salami, green pepper and sprinkle with pepperoni. Repeat layers one more time. Place top of the bread over layered filling.
Serves 4 to 6

LIVERWURST AND ONION SANDWICHES

1/4 pound softened butter
1/4 teaspoon horseradish, well drained
12 slices dark bread
8 ounces sliced liverwurst
1 large red onion, sliced paper thin
1 cucumber, peeled and sliced thin
black pepper
lettuce

Whip the softened butter with the horseradish. Spread on the dark bread, top with liverwurst, onion and cucumber slices. Finish with a grinding of black pepper and lettuce if desired. Best on dark, Italian and French breads.
Makes 6 sandwiches

CHEESE AND GREEN PEPPER SANDWICHES

2 cups grated sharp cheddar cheese
1/2 cup minced green pepper
2 tablespoons chopped green onion
2 tablespoons minced pimiento
mayonnaise
shredded iceberg lettuce
tomato or avocado slices (optional)

Combine grated cheese, green pepper, green onion and pimiento. Blend in enough mayonnaise to bind. Spread on bread, top with shredded lettuce and if desired tomato and/or avocado. (Forget the avocado unless you are assembling the sandwich on picnic location.) Canned green chilies (seeds removed) to taste can replace the green pepper. Carry in cooler chest.
Makes 6 sandwiches

CORNED BEEF AND HORSERADISH SANDWICH

1 3-ounce package softened cream cheese
1 to 2 tablespoons mayonnaise
1 teaspoon Dijon-style mustard
1 to 2 tablespoons chopped parsley
1 to 2 tablespoons well-drained
prepared horseradish
dark or rye bread
corned beef, thinly sliced

Combine all ingredients and blend to create smooth spreading consistency. Spread a thin layer on slices of dark or rye bread. Top with thin slices of corned beef. Serve with dill pickles and beer.
Makes 6 to 8 sandwiches

DANISH MODERN

3 ounces softened cream cheese
dark rye bread
salt and pepper
1/2 pound smoked salmon, thinly sliced
3 hard-boiled eggs, sliced
1 sweet red onion, sliced paper thin
dill weed
lettuce

Spread cream cheese on dark bread. Lightly salt and pepper to taste. Place a few thin strips of smoked salmon over the creamed cheese. Arrange egg and onion slices alternately on top. Garnish with dill and lettuce. For picnics, tote the ingredients in a cooler chest and assemble them on location. Delicious with bagels, French or Italian bread.
Serves 4

Once if I remember well,
my life was a feast
where all hearts opened
and all wines flowed.
—Rimbaud, 1873

HOMEMADE PEANUT BUTTER

1 pound salted, shelled, freshly roasted peanuts
salt to taste

Pour approximately 1/2 cup of peanuts at a time into an electric blender, or just enough to cover the blades. Whirl until a smooth paste. Stop the motor and remove the peanut butter from the container with a rubber scraper. Repeat process until all of the peanuts are used. Add salt to taste. Store in a jar with a tight-fitting lid.

PEANUT BUTTER,
BACON AND CARROT SPREAD

1/2 cup peanut butter
1 cup finely shredded carrots
4 slices bacon, diced, cooked crisp
2 to 3 tablespoons mayonnaise
1 tomato, sliced paper thin
lettuce

Combine peanut butter, shredded carrots and cooked bacon bits. Spread on whole-wheat bread with a thin layer of mayonnaise; top with slices of tomato and lettuce.
Makes 6 sandwiches

PEANUT BUTTER,
CARROT AND RAISIN SPREAD

1/3 cup raisins
1/3 cup orange juice
1-1/2 cups shredded carrots
1 cup peanut butter

Plump the raisins in the orange juice and set aside. In a bowl combine the shredded carrots and peanut butter. Blend in the raisins and the orange juice. Serve on whole-wheat bread.
Makes 4 to 6 sandwiches

APRICOT-NUT SPREAD

1-1/2 cups diced dried apricots
1/3 cup firmly packed brown sugar
1 cup orange juice (or water)
1 cup finely chopped walnuts or your choice
1/3 cup currants (optional)

Combine apricots, sugar and orange juice or water in a saucepan. Cover and simmer over moderate heat for 25 to 30 minutes or until soft and moisture evaporates. Remove from the heat and mash. Add nuts. Stir in currants if you desire a more chutney-like spread. Will keep in refrigerator for several weeks. Use spread as you would jam. It is delicious on any dark breads and on raisin bread. For variation spread the bread with cream cheese or peanut butter and top with apricot-nut spread.
Makes 1-1/2 cups

BEAN AND BACON SPREAD

1 cup cooked baked beans
4 slices diced bacon, cooked crisp
cheddar cheese slices
sliced tomatoes
lettuce

Combine mashed baked beans with crumbled crisp bacon. Spread on whole-wheat or rye bread with or without mayonnaise. Top with cheese, slices of tomato and lettuce.
Makes 4 to 5 sandwiches

HAM AND EGG SPREAD

2/3 to 1 cup minced cooked ham
3 hard-boiled eggs, chopped
1 teaspoon Dijon-style mustard
2 tablespoons minced green onions
2 to 3 tablespoons mayonnaise
salt and pepper to taste

Combine minced ham, chopped egg, mustard and green onions with just enough mayonnaise to bind. Salt and pepper to taste.
Makes 8 to 10 full-size sandwiches

CANTONESE-STYLE TUNA SPREAD

1 7-ounce can tuna, well drained
4 tablespoons chopped chutney
3 tablespoons minced green pepper
3 tablespoons minced green onions
1/2 cup mayonnaise

In a bowl flake the well-drained tuna. Mix in the remaining ingredients and blend thoroughly. Chill in covered container. Serve on white or raisin bread.
Makes 4 to 5 sandwiches

SALMON SPREAD

1 cup flaked cooked salmon
1/4 teaspoon salt
1/4 teaspoon pepper
1/3 cup minced green pepper
1/4 cup minced green onions
1 tablespoon lemon juice
2 to 3 tablespoons mayonnaise
watercress
cucumber slices

Combine the flaked cooked salmon, salt, pepper, green pepper, minced onions, lemon juice and just enough mayonnaise to bind. Garnish with watercress and cucumber slices. Delicious on dark or rye type of breads.
Makes 6 to 8 sandwiches

RELISHES AND FINGER FOODS

Garnish your traveling meals with relishes and finger foods. Take along celery, carrot, cucumber and green pepper sticks, radishes, pickles, olives, cherry tomatoes, cold artichokes, asparagus, marinated or raw mushrooms, cubed cheddar cheese speared with pineapple and olives stuffed with cheese. These garnishes make the difference between a dull appetite and a hearty one!

THERMOS TREATS AND BEVERAGES

Thermos treats are anything that will pour with the exception of carbonated beverages. If a carbonated beverage is added to a punch, for instance, take it along separately and combine it just before serving.

Taking along canned soft drinks raises the question of throw-away cans and bottles versus returnable containers. This is a major concern in regard to the environment. Department and hardware stores offer a wide selection of vacuumed thermos containers, safely designed for transporting contents. Wide-mouthed jars will carry creamy chowders, spaghetti, thick soups, casseroles and chili beans.

Remember a vacuumed container is effective up to four to six hours. To keep hot things hot, heat the inside of the thermos with boiling water for several hours before filling it. And chill an open thermos in the refrigerator for several hours before filling it with cold beverages.

OLD-FASHIONED LEMONADE

1 cup sugar
5 cups cold water
lemon peel from 2 lemons
3/4 cup fresh lemon juice
(approximately 8 lemons)

In a saucepan combine the sugar and 1 cup of the water along with the lemon peelings. Simmer gently for 6 to 8 minutes. Set aside to cool. Strain into the serving pitcher. Add the fresh lemon juice and water, then chill.
Makes 1-1/2 quarts

TROPICAL TEA

4 cups boiling water
2 tablespoons tea leaves
3/4 cup sugar
2-1/2 cups pineapple juice
1 cup cold water
1/4 cup lemon juice
pineapple spears, for garnish (optional)

Pour boiling water over the tea leaves and steep 6 to 8 minutes. Strain. Add the sugar and stir until completely dissolved. Add pineapple juice, water and the lemon juice, mixing thoroughly. Chill. Serve garnished with a spear of pineapple.
Makes 1/2 gallon

HOT CHOCOLATE

2 1-ounce squares unsweetened chocolate,
  broken into pieces
1 cup water
pinch of salt
1/3 cup sugar
3 cups hot milk
marshmallows
1-1/2 teaspoons vanilla extract

Combine chocolate and water in a 2-quart saucepan. Stir over low heat until chocolate has melted and the mixture is smooth. Add salt, sugar and vanilla extract. Gradually blend in the hot milk stirring all the while. Remove from the heat and mix with an egg beater until light and frothy. Pour into thermos. Top with marshmallows just before drinking.
Serves 6

RUSSIAN CHOCOLATE

To the above recipe add 1-1/2 cups rich, hot, strong black coffee. Serve hot or chill and pour over crushed ice.
Serves 8

MINTED ICED TEA

1 lemon
2 oranges
1 handful fresh mint leaves and stalks
  (approximately 15 leaves)
2 tablespoons tea leaves
4 cups boiling water
1 cup sugar cubes or more to taste

First squeeze juice from the lemon and oranges. Set aside. In a bowl place lemon and orange rind cut in strips, mint and tea leaves. Pour boiling water over them and let this steep until water has cooled. Strain. Add the fresh lemon and orange juice, sugar to taste, stirring until sugar dissolves. Chill.
Serves 4

ICY AVGOLEMONO (LEMON SOUP)

8 cups rich chicken broth
4 eggs
juice of 2 lemons
salt and pepper to taste

Heat chicken broth and simmer 15 to 20 minutes. Beat eggs and lemon juice together until well blended. Gradually beat 1 cup of the hot soup into the beaten egg and lemon mixture. Then slowly pour this combination back into the soup pot, continuing to beat. *Do not allow to boil;* heat until slightly thickened. Season with salt and pepper. Cool and then chill. Pour into *well-chilled* vacuumed jugs.
Serves 8

SENEGALESE (COLD CURRY) SOUP

1-1/2 tablespoons cornstarch
1 to 1-1/2 teaspoons curry powder
1-1/2 cups rich chicken broth
1-1/2 cups cream, room temperature
1/2 cup diced cooked chicken

In a saucepan place the cornstarch and curry. Slowly stir in the cold chicken broth. Heat until the soup is just beginning to boil. Remove from the heat and blend in the cream. Set soup aside to cool. Chill thoroughly. Last, stir in the diced cooked chicken. Pour into well-chilled thermos.
Serves 4

VEGETABLE SOUP

4 tablespoons butter
1 tablespoon vegetable oil
1 medium onion, chopped
2 medium carrots, peeled and grated
1 small turnip, peeled and cubed
2 leeks, chopped
1/4 cup chopped parsley
2 stalks celery, chopped
1 medium tomato, peeled and cubed
1 teaspoon salt
pepper to taste
1 teaspoon sugar
2 cups rich beef or chicken broth
1/2 cup cooked peas

In a soup kettle melt the butter and add the oil. Sauté the onion until just turning golden. Add the carrots, turnip, leeks, parsley, celery and sauté a few minutes longer. Stir in the tomato, salt, pepper and sugar. Add stock and simmer for 30 to 40 minutes. Add the cooked peas during the last 5 minutes so that they do not overcook and they retain their bright green color. Pour into preheated thermos.
Serves 4 to 6

WINTER DAY REVIVER

4 cups rich chicken broth
3 cups clam broth
3 cups water
2 tablespoons tomato purée
1 tablespoon chopped parsley
dash Tabasco
1/2 cup dry sherry

Combine chicken broth, clam broth, water and tomato purée in a saucepan. Heat and simmer 15 to 20 minutes. Remove from the heat; stir in the parsley, Tabasco and sherry. Pour into preheated thermos.
Serves 8

PUMPKIN SOUP

3 cups rich chicken broth
2 tomatoes, peeled, seeded and chopped
1 onion, chopped very fine
pinch garlic powder
1/8 teaspoon powdered ginger
1 teaspoon salt
1 cup cooked pumpkin purée
1 cup milk

Combine all ingredients, *except the milk*, in a saucepan. Bring to a boil and simmer gently for 20 minutes. Gradually blend in the milk and heat. Do not boil. Pour into preheated thermos.
Serves 4

CORN CHOWDER

3 slices salt pork (or 1/2 pound bacon), diced
1 large onion, chopped
sprig parsley
1 teaspoon salt
1/4 teaspoon pepper
pinch garlic (optional)
1/4 teaspoon marjoram
pinch powdered sage
1 cup grated raw potato
2 cups rich chicken broth
1/4 cup flour
1/4 cup milk
2 cups corn kernels
1/2 cup additional milk

In a kettle sauté the diced salt pork or bacon until crisp and lightly browned. Pour off excess grease. Stir in the onion and parsley and sauté slightly; do not allow onion to brown. Add seasonings, potato and chicken stock and simmer gently for 15 to 20 minutes. Blend flour into 1/4 cup milk and add to the soup. Stir in the corn and additional milk. Simmer gently 8 to 10 minutes. Pour into preheated thermos.
Serves 4 to 6

Nature never did betray
The heart that loved her.
—William Wordsworth: Tintern Abbey, 1798

WINE CONSOMMÉ

4 cups beef broth
1 cup dry, red wine
1 teaspoon lemon juice

Heat beef broth with red wine. Just before serving stir in 1 teaspoon lemon juice. Pour into preheated thermos. If desired serve with garlic croutons.
Serves 4

TOMATO SOUP

2 tablespoons butter
1 medium onion, chopped
1 large carrot, grated
4 cups rich beef broth
1 large potato, peeled and cubed
2 large tomatoes, peeled and cut up
salt and pepper to taste
pinch marjoram and oregano

Melt the butter in a soup kettle. Sauté the onion and carrot lightly; do not allow it to brown. Pour in the beef broth; add potato, tomatoes, salt, pepper and seasonings. Simmer gently 25 to 30 minutes. If you wish soup to be smooth rather than chunky, allow it to cool and then whirl it in blender. Reheat and pour into heated thermos.
Serves 4 to 6

TOMATO ONION SOUP

2 cups peeled and diced tomatoes
1 clove garlic, minced
1 medium onion, sliced
6 cups rich beef broth

In an electric blender whirl the tomatoes and garlic until smooth. Sauté the sliced onion in butter until a nice light brown. Add the tomato mixture and the beef broth and simmer 20 minutes. Pour into preheated thermos. If served at home, cabin or galley, serve it with grated cheese.
Serves 6 to 8

FIESTA ZUCCHINI SOUP

2 tablespoons olive oil
1/4 cup chopped onion
2 cups chicken broth
dash Tabasco
pinch oregano
4 cups sliced zucchini
1 ripe tomato, peeled and chopped
1/2 teaspoon salt
1/4 cup uncooked rice

In a saucepan heat the oil and sauté the chopped onion until transparent. Add the chicken broth, Tabasco, oregano, sliced zucchini and tomato. Bring to a boil, stir in the rice, and simmer gently for 20 minutes. Pour into preheated thermos.
Serves 4

CHILI CON CARNE

1 pound red pinto beans
1 pound lean ground beef
1 tablespoon bacon grease
2 medium onions, chopped
2 cloves garlic, minced
2 tablespoons flour
1-1/2 teaspoons salt
1 teaspoon oregano
1/2 teaspoon ground cumin
1 tablespoon chili powder, or to taste
1/2 teaspoon ground coriander (optional)
2 tablespoons tomato paste

Precook the beans according to the package directions and reserve the liquid in which they were cooked. In a skillet sauté the beef in bacon grease. Drain off excess fat and push meat to the side. Brown the chopped onions in the bacon grease until just golden; then stir in the garlic and flour. Cook for a few minutes, reduce the heat and pour in the 2 cups of reserved bean liquid and the cooked beans, salt, seasonings and tomato paste. Simmer for 30 minutes. Add more reserved bean liquid or water if necessary. Pour into individual, preheated wide-mouthed thermosware. Serve with cornbread, corn tortillas, or corn chips.
Serves 6

MACARONI AND CHEESE

3 tablespoons butter
1 small onion, minced
1/3 cup minced celery
1/4 cup minced green pepper (optional)
4 cups cooked macaroni (8-ounce package)
1-1/2 cups extra-sharp cubed cheddar cheese
1/4 teaspoon salt
1/4 teaspoon pepper
2 large eggs
3 cups milk

In a skillet melt the butter and lightly sauté the minced onion, celery and green pepper; do not allow it to brown. Turn into a bowl; combine with the cooked macaroni, cubed cheese, salt and pepper. Beat eggs and milk together and pour over the macaroni. Bake at 350° 40 to 45 minutes. Spoon into wide-mouthed thermosware. This casserole can also be wrapped in several thicknesses of newspaper and kept warm several hours for a picnic.
Serves 6

CHEF'S MACARONI SALAD

2 cups cooked, cooled macaroni
(1 cup uncooked)
1-1/2 to 2 cups thin strips cold, cooked meat
(ham, beef tongue, turkey, salami, chicken, etc.)
1/2 cup thin strips cheddar cheese
1/2 cup thin strips Swiss cheese
1/2 cup chopped green onions
1/4 cup chopped pimiento
1/2 cup chopped celery
1/4 cup minced green pepper
3/4 to 1 cup mayonnaise

In a large bowl combine and mix all ingredients in the order given, using just enough mayonnaise to bind. Serve chilled or spoon into prechilled wide-mouthed thermosware.
Serves 6

SPRINGTIME POTATO SALAD

4 cups cubed cooked potatoes, still warm
2 cups cubed cooked leftover lamb,
all fat trimmed off
2 to 3 tablespoons French dressing
1/2 teaspoon salt
ground pepper to taste
2 scallions, chopped
1/4 cup chopped fresh mint
2 teaspoons Dijon-style mustard
3/4 cup mayonnaise

Combine cooked potatoes and meat in a bowl. Pour on dressing, toss gently and allow to marinate until the potatoes have cooled. Add the rest of the ingredients in the order given. Cover and chill.
For Box and Pail: Spoon individual servings into prechilled wide-mouthed thermosware.
At Cabin, in Galley or Camper: Can be served warm or chilled.
For Picnics: Must be taken refrigerated.
Serves 4 to 6

MIXED BEAN SALAD

2 cups cooked kidney beans, drained
1-1/2 cups cooked garbanzo beans, drained
1 cup cooked green beans, drained
1/2 cup chopped celery
1/4 cup chopped green onions
1/4 cup chopped parsley
2 tablespoons chopped pimiento
1 cup French dressing
1/2 cup small cubes Monterey Jack cheese

Place all the ingredients, except for the cubed cheese, into a large container with a tight-fitting lid. Marinate in French dressing for several hours or overnight. Drain, toss with cubed cheese and pack for traveling. A cup of caulifloweretes can replace the cheese for variation and added crunch.
Serves 8 to 10

DELUXE WALDORF SALAD

1/4 cup currants
2 large red-skinned apples
1/2 cup chopped celery
2 tablespoons French dressing
1/4 cup chopped pecans
enough mayonnaise to bind

Plump the currants in a bit of warm water and then drain. Core and cut the apples into bite-size cubes (leave the skins on). Toss with the balance of the ingredients and mix well. Refrigerate, covered with plastic. Spoon into prechilled wide-mouthed thermosware.
Serves 4

The world is a beautiful book,
but of little use to him who cannot read it.
—Carlo Goldoni: Pamela nubile, I, 1757

DESSERTS

Perfect for the box and pail are fruits and cheeses of all kinds, dried fruits such as dates, prunes, figs, raisins, apricots, cookies, cupcakes, nuts and graham crackers. Cakes that travel best are sponge cake, angel food cake, pound cake, fruit cake and any cake or cookie that does not break or crumble easily.

SHORTBREAD COOKIES

1/2 pound softened butter
1/2 cup sugar
1-1/2 teaspoons vanilla extract
2 cups unbleached white flour
1/2 cup flaked angel-type coconut

Cream together soft butter and sugar. Add vanilla. Blend in flour and coconut. Turn stiff dough out onto floured, waxed paper, knead and press together to form into 2 rolls. Wrap in waxed paper and chill 1-1/2 hours. Cut into 1/4-inch slices. Bake on ungreased cookie sheet at 350° for 15 to 20 minutes or until light tan. Sift with powdered sugar while the cookies are still warm.
Makes approximately 3 dozen cookies

BANANA OATMEAL COOKIES

1 cup mashed ripe banana
2 teaspoons orange or lemon juice
1/4 pound softened butter
1 cup sugar
2 eggs
1-1/2 cups sifted unbleached flour
1 teaspoon baking powder
1/4 teaspoon baking soda
1/2 teaspoon salt
1/2 teaspoon nutmeg
1-1/2 cups uncooked rolled oats
1 to 2 tablespoons wheat germ (optional)
2 teaspoons grated orange or lemon rind

Mix mashed banana with orange or lemon juice and set aside. Cream together the butter and sugar until light and fluffy; then beat in the eggs and banana mixture. Stir together flour, baking powder, soda, salt and nutmeg and add to butter, beating until smooth. Fold in the rolled oats, wheat germ and grated orange or lemon rind. Drop by level tablespoon onto lightly greased baking sheets. Bake at 375° for 10 to 12 minutes. These are a soft-textured cookie.
Makes 4 dozen

OATMEAL SPICE COOKIES

3/4 cup softened butter
1 cup brown sugar, firmly packed
1 egg
1/4 cup light molasses
1 teaspoon vanilla extract
1-1/2 cups unbleached white flour
1-1/2 teaspoons baking soda
1/2 teaspoon salt
1 teaspoon each cinnamon and powdered ginger
2-1/2 cups uncooked rolled oats

Cream butter with the sugar. Blend in the egg, molasses and vanilla. Sift flour with soda, salt, cinnamon and ginger; then add to creamed mixture until thoroughly blended. Stir in the oats. Drop by level tablespoon on lightly greased cookie sheets, about 3 inches apart. Bake at 350° for 8 to 10 minutes or until browned. Cool 1 minute on the pan, then remove to wire racks to cool.
Variation: Add 3 teaspoons grated orange peel and 1 cup currants.
Makes 3-1/2 to 4 dozen cookies

HONEY-FRUIT GRAHAM BARS

2 eggs, room temperature
3/4 cup honey
1/2 cup unbleached white flour, sifted
1/2 cup finely crushed graham-cracker crumbs
1 cup snipped dates (or figs or prunes or currants)
pinch of salt
1 cup chopped nuts

Beat eggs until light, gradually adding the honey. Add sifted flour; then the cracker crumbs, dates, nuts and a pinch of salt. Stir in chopped nuts and combine all ingredients thoroughly. Turn into a well-greased 8-inch square pan. Bake at 350° for 30 to 35 minutes or until a toothpick inserted comes out clean. Cut into serving-size squares while still warm.
Makes 1-1/2 to 2 dozen squares

MOCHA BARS

4 tablespoons butter
1 cup brown sugar, firmly packed
1 egg, room temperature
1 cup unbleached white sifted flour
1/2 teaspoon salt
1 teaspoon baking powder
1/4 cup extra-strong, cold black coffee
1-1/2 teaspoons vanilla extract
1/2 cup semisweet chocolate chips
1/2 cup finely chopped nuts

In a saucepan melt butter; then add brown sugar and stir until sugar dissolves. Set aside to cool; then beat egg into cooled mixture. Sift together flour, salt and baking powder and add to butter-egg mixture alternately with the cold coffee. Blend in the vanilla extract and stir in the chocolate chips and nuts. Turn into a well-greased 9-inch baking pan. Bake at 350° for 25 to 30 minutes or until a toothpick inserted comes out clean. Cut into serving-size squares while still warm.
Makes 2-1/2 to 3 dozen bars

CHOCOLATE CHIP SQUARES

1/4 pound softened butter
1/3 cup brown sugar, packed
3 teaspoons grated orange rind
1-1/2 teaspoons vanilla extract
1 egg, separated
1 cup unbleached white flour, sifted
1/4 cup orange juice
1 cup chocolate chips
additional 1/4 cup brown sugar
powdered sugar

Cream together the butter and sugar until light. Blend in the orange rind, vanilla extract and the egg *yolk.* Add the flour alternately with the orange juice. Fold in the chocolate chips. Separately beat the egg white until stiff, gradually beating in the additional cup of brown sugar. Fold into the cookie dough. Spread dough evenly in a greased, paper-lined 8-inch-square baking pan. Bake at 375° for 25 to 30 minutes. While warm dust generously with sifted powdered sugar.
Makes 12 to 14 squares

PEANUT-BUTTER HONEY CRISPS

1/4 pound softened butter
1/2 cup peanut butter, creamy or chunk style
1/2 cup honey
1/2 cup brown sugar, firmly packed
1 egg, room temperature
2 cups sifted unbleached white flour
1/2 teaspoon baking soda
1/4 teaspoon salt

Cream butter and peanut butter together. Blend in the honey and brown sugar, beating until light and fluffy. Add the egg. Sift dry ingredients and blend into peanut-butter mixture. Form into balls, place on a lightly greased baking sheet and press flat with fork tines. Bake at 350° for 8 to 10 minutes.
Makes 3-1/2 to 4 dozen crisps

STAMP AND GO DESSERT BARS

1/4 pound butter
1 cup graham-cracker crumbs
3/4 cup shredded coconut
1 cup walnuts, chopped fine
6 ounces semisweet chocolate chips
(or butterscotch flavored)
1-1/3 cups condensed milk

Melt the butter in a 13x9x2-inch baking pan. Over the butter, evenly sprinkle the graham-cracker crumbs. Next sprinkle on the coconut, chopped nuts and the candy chips. Over this pour the condensed milk carefully and evenly. Bake at 350° for 20 minutes. Cool and cut into small squares.
Makes 2-1/2 to 3 dozen squares

GINGERBREAD

1/2 cup dark full-flavored molasses
3/4 cup boiling water
4 tablespoons softened butter
1/2 teaspoon baking soda
1/2 cup sugar
1/4 teaspoon salt
1/2 teaspoon powdered ginger
1 teaspoon cinnamon
1-1/2 cups unbleached white flour
1-1/2 teaspoons baking powder
1 egg, beaten

In a large bowl combine molasses, boiling water, butter and baking soda. Sift sugar salt, ginger, cinnamon, flour and baking powder. Blend in dry ingredients alternately with molasses mixture, then blend in beaten egg. Batter will be thin. Pour into a greased and lightly floured 11x7x1-1/2-inch pan or a 9x9-inch pan. Bake at 350° for 30 to 35 minutes or until a toothpick inserted comes out clean.
Serves 6 to 8

BANANA BREAD

1-1/2 cups sifted unbleached white flour
1/2 teaspoon baking soda
1/2 teaspoon baking powder
1/2 teaspoon salt
3/4 cup mashed bananas (1-1/2 to 2 bananas)
2 tablespoons orange juice
1/2 cup shortening
3/4 cup sugar
2 eggs
1 teaspoon vanilla extract
1 teaspoon grated orange rind

Sift flour, soda, baking powder and salt. In another bowl whip the mashed banana with the orange juice. Cream shortening and sugar together until smooth; then beat in the eggs, adding vanilla extract and grated orange rind. Stir in dry ingredients alternately with whipped banana mixture. Pour into 9x5x3-inch greased loaf pan. Bake at 350° for 1 hour or until a toothpick inserted comes out clean. Allow to set 10 minutes then remove from the pan to cool on a cake rack.
Serves 6

ALMOND POUND CAKE

1/2 pound softened butter
2-1/2 cups sugar
4 eggs
3 cups sifted unbleached white flour
1/4 teaspoon baking soda
1 cup buttermilk
1/2 teaspoon vanilla extract
1-1/2 teaspoons almond extract

In a mixing bowl whip the butter until light and creamy. Gradually work in the sugar, mixing after each addition; then beat in the eggs, one at a time. Sift flour and soda together and add it alternately with the buttermilk to the butter mixture. Last, blend in the extracts. Pour into a greased and floured 10-inch tube pan. Bake at 350° for 1 hour and 15 minutes or until a toothpick inserted comes out clean. Allow the cake to set 10 minutes before removing from the pan. Invert onto a wire cake rack to cool.

Variation, Almond Chocolate: Add 2/3 cup ground cocoa.
Serves 10

Carefree and Impromptu Picnics

For lo the winter is past,
the rain is over and gone;
The flowers appear on the earth;
the time of the singing of birds is come,
and the voice of the turtle is heard in our land;
The fig tree putteth forth her green figs,
and the vines with the tender grape give a good smell.
Arise, my love, my fair one, and come away.
—Song of Solomon 2:11-13

Carefree and Impromptu Picnics

PICNICS

Picnics can happen quite unexpectedly. Although you cannot always prepare for them, *The Portable Feast* makes suggestions for one of two possibilities: the improvised picnic from the kitchen or the improvised picnic en route. The first can be solved with the following ideas and recipes; the second, however, can be solved with only a few suggestions.

If you're inclined toward this type of event, keep your car equipped with can/bottle opener, corkscrew, knife, plastic glasses and napkins. Your only concern after that is to find the nearest supermarket or delicatessen. The quickest and easiest is an assortment of cheeses, nuts, crackers, breads, canned pâté, smoked salmon, marinated mushrooms or artichokes and fruit or vegetables. A European-style picnic consisting of bread, cheese, salami, fruit and wine is always a pleasure.

There are many prepared dips such as garlic, onion or avocado which make excellent bread spreads, and there are prepared salads, assorted cold cuts and cheeses. And, of course, you can always succumb to caviar on plain crackers washed down with champagne!

Impromptu portable meals can originate wherever you are. The recipes in this chapter are convenient, unusual combinations, made in a very short time. Give them a try!

PICNIC BASICS FOR STOCKING THE KITCHEN

The following culinary basics are all that is necessary to be ready for an impromptu, portable feast.

Bacon: canned Danish or fresh
Beans: canned baked, kidney, garbanzo, etc.
Breads: homemade, white, wheat, French (keep a few extra loaves frozen)
Butter
Cheese: cheddar, Monterey, Swiss, Parmesan, Mozzarella, cream cheese
Cocoa: chocolate, semisweet, unsweetened
Coffee: fresh ground, instant
Condiments: catsup, chili sauce, Dijon-style mustard, soy sauce, Worcestershire sauce, pickle relish
Cookies
Crackers: variety
Cream: dry and canned
Eggs
Fish: canned tuna, salmon, crab, shrimp, oysters, clams, sardines
Freeze dried: chives and green pepper
Fruit: canned and dry: raisins, prunes, figs, apricots
Herbs
Lemons: fresh
Mayonnaise
Meat: canned tongue, ham, corned beef hash, chipped beef
Nuts: sunflower seeds, sesame seeds, cashews
Oil: corn oil, peanut oil, olive oil
Olives: sliced, chopped, pimiento-stuffed
Onions: fresh, dried, powdered
Pasta: assortment of dry, frozen
Pepper: black ground pepper, green pepper (dehydrated) and white pepper
Pickles: relishes
Pimientos: jar or canned
Potatoes: fresh, dehydrated
Soups: variety canned and dry packaged
Sugar: lumps, granulated, powdered, brown (small packets)
Tea: herb, spice
Tomatoes: fresh
Wines: red, white, sherry, port (for drinking and cooking)

APPROXIMATE RECIPE SUBSTITUTIONS

Here is a list of alternatives that can be helpful when you are out of some basic ingredient. Check these suggestions for recipe substitutions.

Arrowroot 1 tablespoon = 2 tablespoons regular flour
Cornstarch 1 tablespoon = 2 tablespoons regular flour
Baking powder 1 teaspoon = 1/4 teaspoon baking soda plus 1/2 teaspoon cream of tartar or 1/4 teaspoon baking soda plus 1/2 cup buttermilk or 1/4 teaspoon baking soda plus 1/3 cup molasses
Baking soda Use with sour milk, buttermilk, sour cream, fruit juices, chocolate and sometimes with molasses. With sour milk, buttermilk or sour cream, use 1/2 teaspoon baking soda and *reduce* baking powder called for by 2 teaspoons.
Sour milk 1 cup = lukewarm fresh milk less 1 tablespoon plus 1 tablespoon vinegar and allow to stand 5 minutes. Can be used in place of buttermilk.
Potato flour 1 tablespoon = 2 tablespoons regular flour
Flour 1 tablespoon = 1-1/2 teaspoons cornstarch, or 3/4 tablespoon quick-cooking tapioca
Unbleached white flour 1 cup = 1 cup cornmeal
Sifted all-purpose flour 1 cup = 1-1/8 cups (1 cup plus 2 tablespoons) sifted *cake* flour
Sifted cake flour 1 cup = 7/8 cup (1 cup minus 2 tablespoons) sifted all-purpose flour
Unsweetened chocolate 1 square = 1 ounce = 3 tablespoons cocoa plus 1 tablespoon fat (i.e. butter)
Butter 1 cup = 1 cup margarine or 7/8 cup lard plus 1/2 teaspoon salt or 7/8 cup hydrogenated fat plus 1/2 teaspoon salt
Cream substitute 1/3 cup powdered milk to 1/2 cup water for coffee. In recipes use: 3 tablespoons butter plus 3/4 cup milk or 1/3 cup butter plus 3/4 cup milk.
Eggs In recipes requiring egg yolks only, whole eggs can be substituted. Use 1 whole egg for each 2 yolks.
Herbs 1/2 to 1-1/2 teaspoons dry herbs = 1 tablespoon fresh herbs
Yogurt 1 cup = 1 cup buttermilk
Corn syrup 1 cup = 1 cup sugar plus 1/4 cup liquid
Honey 1 cup = 1 to 1-1/4 cups sugar plus 1/4 cup liquid; 1/2 cup = 3/4 cup sugar plus 1/8 cup liquid
Brown sugar 1 cup firmly packed = 1 cup granulated white sugar
Confectioners sugar 1-3/4 cups packed = 1 cup granulated white sugar
Garlic powder 1/8 teaspoon = 1 small clove fresh garlic
Fresh milk 1 cup = 1/2 cup evaporated milk plus 1/2 cup water, but you must reduce the sugar in the recipe. Or 4 tablespoons powdered skim milk plus 2 tablespoons butter, plus 1 cup water.

A DO-IT-YOURSELF SMORGASBORD

prosciutto or pastrami, sliced
Provolone cheese, sliced
red onion, sliced paper thin
Canadian bacon, sliced paper thin
Monterey Jack cheese, sliced
Swiss cheese, sliced
roast beef, sliced thin
cucumbers, peeled, sliced thin
tomatoes, sliced thin
avocado, peeled, sliced thin
assorted lettuce
assorted pickles and olives
smoked salmon, sliced thin
turkey, sliced thin
Bread spreads
soft butter
horseradish
Dijon-style mustard
mayonnaise
any of the following spreads
Breads
homemade

FRENCH CAPER PÂTÉ

4 to 5 slices bacon, fried crisp and crumbled
1 pound braunschweiger (smoked liverwurst)
1 8-ounce package softened cream cheese
1 3-ounce package blue cheese, crumbled
1/4 cup drained capers
3 hard-boiled eggs, sieved
French rolls or loaf

Combine all ingredients (except bread) thoroughly until smooth and well blended. Chill until serving time. Spread on French bread and wrap for packing or take ingredients to the picnic location. Serve with wine, a fresh green salad and fresh fruit for dessert.
Serves 4 to 6

QUICK PÂTÉ

1/2 pound braunschweiger (smoked liverwurst)
1/2 cup sour cream or mayonnaise
1/2 teaspoon Worcestershire sauce
3 to 4 teaspoons grated onion
2 to 3 tablespoons cognac or vermouth

Cream all ingredients together or mix in an electric blender. Put into container with tight-fitting lid and chill. Spread on dark or rye bread or crackers. Serve with wine.
Serves 4 to 6

Awake, O north wind; and come, thou south;
blow upon my garden, that the spices thereof may flow out.
Let my beloved come into his garden,
and eat his pleasant fruits.
—Song of Solomon 4:16

DEVILED EGG AND SESAME SEED SPREAD

2 tablespoons sesame seeds
4 hard-boiled eggs, chopped
1/2 cup finely chopped celery
3 to 4 tablespoons mayonnaise
1 teaspoon Dijon-style mustard
2 tablespoons minced green onion

Toast the sesame seeds in a shallow pan in a 350° oven, watching closely, for 5 to 8 minutes, shaking the pan occasionally to insure even browning. Combine the rest of the ingredients and blend in the cooled toasted seeds. Serve on French, Italian or whole-wheat breads. Carry in cooler chest.
Makes 6 sandwiches

EGG-BACON-CHEESE FILLING

4 to 6 slices bacon
2 hard-boiled eggs, chopped
1 green onion, minced
2 tablespoons chopped green pepper
2 tablespoons chopped celery
1/2 cup shredded sharp cheddar cheese
3 to 4 tablespoons mayonnaise
lettuce or spinach

Cook bacon until crisp, drain on paper towels, crumble and set bacon bits aside. Combine chopped egg with minced onion, green pepper, celery and shredded cheese. Mix in just enough mayonnaise to bind ingredients together. Spread on bread and sprinkle on the bacon bits. Garnish with lettuce or spinach leaves. Carry in cooler chest.
Makes 2 cups

TUNA, CHEESE AND EGG SPREAD

1 6-1/2-ounce can tuna (packed in water), drained
3 hard-boiled eggs, chopped
1 cup grated cheddar cheese
1/4 cup minced green pepper
1/4 cup minced celery
2 tablespoons minced onion
1 tablespoon sweet-pickle relish, drained
mayonnaise

Combine ingredients and blend thoroughly, adding just enough mayonnaise to bind. Serve on whole-wheat or white bread. Carry in cooler chest.
Makes 8 sandwiches

SARDINE PÂTÉ

2 15-ounce cans sardines, well drained
5 hard-boiled eggs, shredded
1/2 cup minced onion
1 to 2 tablespoons mayonnaise
1 teaspoon Dijon-style mustard
2 to 3 teaspoons lemon juice
sliced cucumbers

In a bowl mash the sardines and blend in the shredded eggs, minced onion, mayonnaise (start with 1 tablespoon and add more if needed), mustard and lemon juice. Chill in covered container. Serve on dark or white bread and top with thin slices of cucumber.
Serves 6 to 8

CREAM CHEESE SPREAD

1 8-ounce package soft cream cheese
1/4 cup sour cream or mayonnaise
pinch of salt and garlic powder
2 teaspoons lemon juice
1/2 teaspoon dill weed

Combine above ingredients in a small bowl and whip or cream to create a smooth spreading consistency. Chill until serving time.

CREAM CHEESE-PECAN SPREAD

8 ounces softened cream cheese
mayonnaise
1/2 cup finely chopped pecans

In a small bowl cream the softened cheese with just enough mayonnaise to form a smooth consistency for spreading, blending in the chopped pecans. Delicious on raisin bread. Carry in cooler chest.
Makes 6 to 8 sandwiches

CHEESE AND BEER SPREAD

2 cups shredded cheddar cheese
4 tablespoons softened butter
1/4 cup beer, room temperature
dash Tabasco
dash Worcestershire sauce

Grate cheese and blend in the softened butter. Add just enough beer to reach the desired spreading consistency. Add Tabasco and Worcestershire to taste. Serve on dark breads. Carry in cooler chest.
Makes approximately 8 sandwiches

CHEDDAR AND OLIVE SPREAD

1/2 pound (2 cups) grated cheddar cheese
1/4 cup minced pimiento-stuffed green olives
1 to 2 tablespoons sherry
2 to 3 tablespoons softened butter

Combine the above ingredients in a bowl to form a smooth spreading consistency. Put on dark breads. Serve with cold beer.
Serves 4 to 6

TUNA-NUT SPREAD

1 6-1/2-ounce can tuna (packed in water), drained
1/4 cup minced parsley
1 tablespoon minced green onion
1/2 cup minced celery
1/2 cup finely chopped walnuts or your choice
mayonnaise

Combine ingredients adding just enough mayonnaise to bind the contents together. Serve on whole-wheat or white bread. Carry in cooler chest.
Makes 6 sandwiches

HUNGARIAN EGG SPREAD

4 hard-boiled eggs, chopped
1/4 cup mayonnaise
1 to 2 teaspoons white wine vinegar
2 teaspoons grated onion
1/2 teaspoon Worcestershire sauce
1 teaspoon Dijon-type mustard
paprika

Blend all ingredients thoroughly and press into a 1-cup container. Chill. Unmold and sprinkle heavily with paprika. Take along chilled in a cooler chest to picnics or spread on rye or dark breads and wrap before packing.
Makes 1 cup

A hare stopped in the clover
and swaying flower bells, and said
a prayer to the rainbow
through the spider's web.
—A. Rimbaud: The Illuminations, 1871

Merum
novos
compesce
dolores,
occupet ut
fessi lumina
victa sopor.

STEAK TARTARE

1 pound raw ground sirloin
1 egg yolk, beaten
1/4 cup minced onion
1 tablespoon well-drained capers
1/2 teaspoon Dijon-style mustard
1 tablespoon olive oil
1 teaspoon Worcestershire sauce
salt and ground pepper to taste
dash Tabasco (optional)

If you happen to have a pound of hamburger, this is a good way to dress it up. Combine above ingredients in a bowl in the order given. Mix thoroughly and form into a loaf. Score and decorate the top with additional capers or anchovies (if desired) and additional minced onions. Wrap and refrigerate.
For Picnics: Keep refrigerated in cooler chest until ready to use. Serve with dark breads and beer.
Serves 6

MEXICAN SANDWICHES DERECHO

4 to 6 crusty French rolls
1 4-ounce can green chilies, peeled and seeded
3/4 cup mayonnaise
10 to 12 slices Monterey Jack cheese
sliced tomatoes
sliced avocado
ripe olives

Slice rolls in half lengthwise. Drain chilies and mash (amount is according to desired spiciness; start with 1 tablespoon.) Blend the mashed chilies with the mayonnaise and spread generously on the cut rolls. Top with cheese and broil 6 inches from the heating unit until hot and bubbly. Garnish just before eating with slices of tomato and avocado. Serve with olives and beer.
For Picnics: Prepare rolls and broil. Wrap each one individually in foil then in several thicknesses of newspaper. Will stay warm for several hours. Or tote them in the cooler chest and reheat them at the picnic location. Place foil-wrapped rolls on a hot grill, or tuck them among the hot coals for a few minutes. Take garnish along separately and add just before serving.
Serves 4

NO-OTHER-CHOICE PICNIC LOAF

1 loaf French or Italian bread
butter
1 pint cottage cheese
1 to 2 green onions, minced
mayonnaise (optional)
2 to 3 slices bacon, fried crisp and crumbled
sliced tomatoes and cucumbers
chopped parsley

Slice the loaf in half lengthwise. Scoop out the loaf. Generously butter the inside to prevent loaf from becoming soggy. Combine the cottage cheese, minced onions, extra bread crumbs and a bit of mayonnaise if desired to make a smooth filling consistency. Stuff and refill the bread, salt and pepper to taste, sprinkle on the crumbled bacon bits and replace the top portion of the bread. Wrap in foil and refrigerate until ready to leave. Garnish with sliced tomatoes, cucumbers and chopped parsley just before serving.
Serves 4 to 6

ONION SANDWICHES

Slice homemade bread thinly. Spread each slice with a fine layer of mayonnaise and a bit of Dijon-style mustard. Top each piece with shreds of sweet red onion. Sprinkle with salt, pepper and minced parsley, then cover with other slices of bread. Serve with cold beer.

RAILROAD SANDWICH
(Recommended by Mozart Kaufman)

Slice loaf of Italian bread in half lengthwise. Scoop out some of the bread and spread on thin amount of mayonnaise if desired. Layer with assorted cheeses and luncheon meats, but avoid tomato and avocado or anything exceptionally juicy. After the sandwich is assembled, wrap it in foil and then a large towel. Ask the children to sit on it en route to the picnic, the entire time. By the time you get there the loaf will be completely flattened like a layered torte. The end results must be flat. Slice crosswise and enjoy!

GYPSY BREAD

1 loaf French or Italian bread
1 cup grated sharp cheddar cheese
1 small onion, chopped
1/3 to 1/2 cup mayonnaise
1 to 2 tablespoons minced green pepper (optional)
2 teaspoons white wine vinegar
1/2 teaspoon curry powder
1/2 cup chopped ripe olives

Slice the loaf of bread lengthwise. Combine the rest of the ingredients into a smooth spreadable consistency. Spread on the bread and broil at least 6 inches from the heating unit until cheese melts.
For Picnics: Prepare as directed. Heat and wrap foil then in several thicknesses of newspaper to keep warm for several hours. Or tote bread in the cooler chest and reheat it at the picnic location. Place foil-wrapped loaf on a hot grill or tuck it among the coals for a few minutes. Pass the red wine.
Serves 4 to 6

LOAF ALLA LAZIO

1 loaf Italian crusty bread (page 24)
4 tablespoons olive oil
4 tablespoons soft butter
dash garlic powder
8 to 10 drained anchovies
2 tablespoons drained capers
sprig parsley, chopped
Mozzarella, Bel Paese or Provolone cheese

Slice the loaf in half lengthwise. In a bowl combine the olive oil, soft butter, garlic powder and mashed anchovies. Cream the ingredients into a smooth paste. Spread on bread. Sprinkle with capers and top with shredded cheese. Eat as is or heat in a 350° oven on a cookie sheet until cheese melts. Serve with sliced tomatoes, Italian pepperonis and rich, red wine like a Barbera.
For Picnics: Prepare as directed. Heat and wrap the loaf in foil, then several thicknesses of newspaper to keep warm for several hours. Or tote loaf in the cooler chest and reheat it at the picnic location. Simply place foil-wrapped loaf on a hot grill or tuck it among the hot coals for a few minutes.
Serves 4 to 6

CHILI RELLENO BAKED PRONTO

1 4-ounce can green peeled and roasted chilies
1 large onion, sliced paper thin
10 ounces extra-sharp cheddar cheese, sliced
4 eggs
2 cups milk
1/2 cup flour
1 teaspoon salt
dash garlic powder (optional)

Wash seeds from the canned chilies and dice into bite-size pieces. In a well-buttered 1-quart casserole, layer the chilies, onion slices and cheese. Beat eggs, milk, flour, seasonings and pour over all. Bake at 350° for 45 to 50 minutes or until custard sets and is puffed and golden.
For Picnics: To bake and take, the instructions are the same as for a quiche. This recipe is also delicious cold. Allow to cool, chill and then take in the cooler chest.
Serves 4 to 6

POOR MAN'S QUICHE

4 slices white bread
softened butter
3 eggs
1-1/2 cups milk
1/2 cup white wine
1/2 teaspoon Dijon-style mustard
1/8 teaspoon nutmeg (optional)
2 cups grated cheese—Swiss or cheddar, etc.
1 green onion, minced, including tops

Spread both sides of each slice of bread with soft butter. Arrange slices in a 9- or 10-inch pie plate or square baking dish to form a crust. Beat the eggs with the milk, wine, mustard and nutmeg. Sprinkle the bread with grated cheese and minced green onions. Pour beaten egg-milk combination over all. Cover with plastic wrap and allow to soak for 30 to 40 minutes. Bake at 350° for 25 to 30 minutes or until puffed and golden.
For Picnics: Cover serving dish with foil and wrap in several thicknesses of newspaper to keep warm for several hours.
Serves 4

BASIC QUICHE

1 chilled pastry shell

Filling #1

4 eggs
2 cups milk
1/4 teaspoon salt
1/8 teaspoon nutmeg
dash white pepper (optional)

Filling #2

3 eggs
3/4 cup milk
1/2 cup sour cream
1/4 teaspoon salt
1/8 teaspoon nutmeg

Quiche Lorraine Put 6 slices of precooked, crumbled bacon on the bottom of the pastry shell. Over the bacon bits sprinkle 1/2 to 1 cup grated Swiss or Gruyère cheese. Combine ingredients in filling #1 or #2 and carefully pour them over the bacon and cheese. Dust with paprika. Bake at 375° for 30 to 35 minutes or until the custard is set, puffed and golden.

Quiche Niçoise Prepare filling #1 or #2. Add 1/4 cup of sautéed onion, 1/4 cup of seasoned tomato sauce, 3 tablespoons chopped parsley, pinch of cayenne pepper or a dash of Tabasco sauce and 1/4 cup chopped ripe olives. Float anchovy filets on top; sprinkle with 1/4 to 1/2 cup of grated Swiss or Gruyère cheese. Bake as directed for Quiche Lorraine.

Seafood Quiche Prepare filling #1 or #2. Add 1-1/2 cups fresh or canned crab, shrimp, lobster or 1 can well-drained minced clams. Blend in 1 tablespoon lemon juice, 2 tablespoons sherry, onion powder or minced green onions, 2 tablespoons catsup (optional) and 3/4 cup shredded Swiss cheese. Bake as for other quiches.

For Picnics: Cover serving dish with foil and wrap in several thicknesses of newspaper to keep warm for several hours.
Serves 6 to 8

SALADS

When faced with impromptu salad preparation you will most likely work with what you have. Select a few complementary combinations and toss with dressing. The only requirement is that salad greens be fresh and crisp. Salads can be made from almost anything: vegetables, fruits, cold diced meats, poultry, seafood and eggs. To top them off, make fresh dressing at the table consisting of olive oil, wine vinegar and a grinding of coarse Java pepper. And for something extra special, check the following list of ideas.

Any kind of salad travels well if you keep these thoughts in mind. Wash, drain and carry lettuce and any other fresh greens in a large plastic container with a tight-fitting lid. Take the other ingredients such as avocados, tomatoes, soft fruits or vegetables and salad dressing separately and add just before serving. After adding the garnish and dressing, replace the lid of the container, then toss gently. Always keep the ingredients refrigerated in the cooler chest; no one enjoys a warm salad.

IDEAS FOR ADDED CRUNCH AND TEXTURE

Apples, alfalfa sprouts, bean sprouts, bacon bits, bamboo shoots, carrots, raw cauliflower, celery, croutons, shredded hard-cooked egg, raw mushrooms, chopped nuts, onion rings, parsley, radishes, scallions, snow peas.

ADDED INTEREST AND THE UNUSUAL

Anchovies, avocado, all kinds of beans, beets, capers, cheese (cubed cream cheese, cubed Monterey Jack, Parmesan), canned, diced roasted chilies (peeled, seeded), coriander (Chinese parsley), cubed corned beef, hearts of palm (canned), Italian flat parsley, ham, turkey, beef tongue (julienne sliced), cooked chilled macaroni, mandarin orange sections, mangos (canned), melon balls (all kinds), mustard and collard greens, nasturtium leaves (tender young ones), olives (all kinds), oysters, papaya, persimmons (peeled and sliced), pickles, pimiento, potatoes (cooked, cubed), raisins (soaked in sherry), rose petals, cubed salami, turnip greens, violets, water chestnuts, sliced raw zucchini.

Oh, for a lodge in some vast wilderness,
Some boundless contiguity of shade,
Where rumor of oppression and deceit,
Of unsuccessful or successful war,
Might never reach me more!
—William Cowper, The Task, 1785

COMPLEMENTARY SALAD COMBINATIONS

Lima beans and celery with minced green onions
Sliced beets with sliced oranges
Cucumbers and sour cream
Bermuda onion slices and orange slices
Melon balls: honeydew, cantaloupe, watermelon with blueberries
Celery, seedless grapes, avocado, tomato wedges
Marinated cauliflower with pimiento, green pepper, ripe olives and minced green onions
Avocado and papaya
Avocado and sliced persimmons with French dressing
Orange sections and chopped fresh mint
Sliced beefsteak tomatoes, splashed with cognac and sprinkled with chives
Shredded carrot, marinated and served in avocado cavity
Ripe olives stuffed with small cubes Jack cheese, with anchovies, in a tossed green salad
Spinach salad with bacon bits and artichoke hearts
Shrimp, mandarin oranges, slivered almonds
Sliced oranges, splashed with brandy, served with onion rings
Cubed chicken, diced celery, apple, seedless grapes and cantaloupe balls
White pearl corn (canned) with minced scallions, chopped olives
Shrimp, scallions, celery, bean sprouts, snow peas with French dressing
Melon balls, pineapple, strawberries, chopped mint, chopped nuts
Cucumbers, radishes, horseradish-flavored sour cream
Cucumber, shrimp, watercress with sherry added to the French dressing
Chinese cabbage with chopped green or red bell pepper, chopped scallions, chopped parsley with mayonnaise dressing
Mint with marinated onion rings
Pineapple with watercress and slivered almonds
Marinated scallops and shrimp, filled avocado with curried mayonnaise
Pears and shredded cheddar cheese
Pears with mandarin oranges and blue cheese dressing
Pepperoni diced, cubed Monterey Jack with tossed green salad
Diced cold potatoes, anchovies, hard-cooked egg wedges, tomatoes and olives
Pineapple chunks, celery, green pepper
Orange and pineapple with dash cinnamon added to a sherry dressing
Kidney beans, onion rings, celery, cubed Monterey Jack

CLASSIC FRENCH VINAIGRETTE DRESSING

2 teaspoons salt
fresh ground pepper
5 tablespoons white wine vinegar
1/4 teaspoon Dijon-style mustard
3/4 cup olive oil
1/4 teaspoon crushed dry tarragon

Blend ingredients in a jar with a tight-fitting lid. Shake well.

LEMON VINAIGRETTE

1/2 cup lemon juice
1 teaspoon salt
1/4 teaspoon ground pepper
1/2 teaspoon sugar or honey
1-1/2 cups olive oil

Blend in a jar with tight-fitting lid in order given. Shake well. Chill.

CAPER DRESSING

1 cup French dressing
1 hard-cooked egg, shredded
1 tablespoon capers, drained
2 tablespoons chopped parsley
1 minced shallot, or a dash of garlic

Combine ingredients in order given. Shake well before using.

RUSSIAN DRESSING

1/2 cup red or white wine vinegar
1/4 cup water
2 tablespoons sugar
1/4 cup catsup
1/2 teaspoon salt
dash garlic powder
1/2 cup olive oil
diced pimiento and green pepper (optional)

Blend in a jar with tight-fitting lid in order given. Shake well. Chill.

ISLAND DRESSING FOR FRUIT SALADS

1 cup French dressing
3 tablespoons chutney
1 teaspoon Dijon-style mustard
1 teaspoon lemon juice

Combine ingredients in order given. Shake well before using.

CITRUS DRESSING FOR FRUIT SALADS

1 cup French dressing
2 tablespoons lemon or orange juice
3 teaspoons honey
1/2 teaspoon grated lemon or orange rind
1 teaspoon grenadine (optional)

Combine ingredients in order given. Shake well before using.

HOT DRESSING

1 cup French dressing
2 to 3 teaspoons horseradish
dash Tabasco sauce
1/2 to 1 teaspoon sugar

Combine ingredients in order given. Shake well before using.

CURRY DRESSING

1 cup French dressing
1/4 to 1/2 teaspoon curry powder
pinch garlic powder
1/8 teaspoon powdered ginger
1/2 to 1 teaspoon soy sauce

Combine ingredients in order given. Shake well before using. Garnish salad with chopped mint and chopped nuts.

CAREFREE AND IMPROMPTU DESSERTS

This section covers simple, tasty, easily transported desserts. The perfect choice for an impromptu dessert is a selection of the season's fresh fruit and assorted cheeses. Should you feel more creative, make a French macédoine, a dessert of various cut-up fruits enhanced with liqueurs. These suggestions are most appropriate and more desirable than a fancy, complicated dessert.

MACÉDOINES

Berries Raspberries and sliced nectarines with framboise

Raspberries and orange sections with Cointreau

Berries(any variety) marinated in kirsch, served over lemon sherbet with pound cake or cookies

Strawberries and pineapple with kirsch, served with a dollop of sour cream and sprinkled with brown sugar

Strawberries with port

Cantaloupe Escoffier Marinate cantaloupe balls, strawberries, pineapple and raspberries in kirsch and top with whipped cream (optional).

Cherries, bing Marinate in kirsch.

Melon balls Pour a sherry or liqueur of your choice over each serving in a cocktail glass. Garnish with mint.

Oranges Marinate sections with grapefruit, in orange liqueur; sprinkle with coconut and toasted almonds.

Orange sections, pineapple, coconut and preserved ginger with Cointreau

Tangerine sections marinated in orange-flavored liqueur, sprinkle with chopped dates. Nice during holidays.

Persimmons Peel and slice crosswise (the firm variety slice best, they are Fuyu, Maru and Hyakume). Sprinkle with sherry.

Peaches Marinate peaches and pears in brandy; glaze with melted currant jelly.

Pears Serve with crème de menthe (white or green) or Cointreau.

Plums Serve stewed plums in a sherbet glass, splash with cognac.

Prunes Stew with spices. Marinate in port or sherry. Serve three in a small glass container. Top with a dollop of sour cream and a twist of lemon peel.

Figs Chill Kadota figs and serve with sour cream and a sprinkling of brown sugar.

Kumquats Serve with cream cheese. Eat the skin and all.

Frosted Grapes Dip small bunches of washed and dried grapes in frothy beaten egg whites. Roll in granulated sugar; set on cake rack to dry. Refrigerate on rack over wax paper on a cookie sheet.

Elegant Picnics

Where there is no wine, love perishes,
and everything else that is pleasant to man.
—Euripides: The Bacchae, c. 410

Elegant Picnics

ELEGANT PICNICS (With Menus and Wine)

The portable feast can range from the simple, impromptu menu, as you have seen, to something more elaborate. This chapter focuses on the luxurious and the elegant. A successful, well-planned menu takes time and effort. It involves foods that can only be considered with the proper picnic equipment to ensure safety as well as taste and quality. With a cooler chest literally any type of foods can be transported. Take along insulated containers for hot and cold food or drink. Although many picnic areas will have a barbecue or campfire, a hibachi or portable grill allows greater mobility. Sophisticated tastes need not remain at home. Include your favorite linen, wine glasses, candelabra and china. Therefore night or day, spring, summer, autumn or winter, indoors, outdoors, just the two of you or with a crowd, celebrate for a truly elegant repast.

PARISIAN FEAST

Barbecued Cornish Game Hens*
Sourdough French Bread (page 19)
Elegant Pâté-Egg Spread*
Summer Salad*
Brie Cheese and Crisp Apples or Pears
Petits Fours (from the bakery)
Suggested wine: Extra Dry Champagne, Pinot Chardonnay or Sauvignon Blanc

*Recipes Follow

ELEGANT PÂTÉ-EGG SPREAD

4 hard-boiled eggs, shredded
1/4 to 1/3 cup imported canned
  pâté de foie gras
2 teaspoons grated onion
1 tablespoon minced parsley
2 tablespoons mayonnaise

Cream together shredded eggs and pâté until smooth and thoroughly blended. Add the grated onion, parsley and mayonnaise. Chill in a covered container. Tote in cooler chest. Spread on French bread.
Serves 4

SUMMER SALAD

1 head cauliflower
1 basket cherry tomatoes
1 pound green beans, sliced diagonally
  and cooked
1 pound carrots, sliced diagonally and cooked
1/2 to 3/4 cup French dressing (page 99)
chopped parsley

Break cauliflower into separate little flowerettes. Drop into boiling water and blanch for 10 to 12 minutes; drain and cool. Stem and wash the cherry tomatoes. Combine flowerettes, cherry tomatoes, green beans, carrots and dressing. Toss gently and refrigerate until served. Garnish with parsley.
Serves 6

BARBECUED CORNISH GAME HENS

4 Cornish game hens
juice of 1 lemon
1/4 pound butter
1/4 cup white wine
1/4 cup minced onion
1/4 cup minced parsley
1/2 teaspoon thyme
salt and pepper to taste

Rub birds with lemon juice and put in enamelware saucepan. Birds can be roasted on grill at picnic site for 50 to 60 minutes and eaten hot. They also can be roasted at home 40 to 50 minutes in 375° oven and eaten cold, or partially roasted at home in 375° oven and then barbecued briefly at the picnic site on grill. Melt butter, add wine, herbs and seasoning just before roasting. Use mixture to baste during roasting or grilling. Game hen is done when the meat pulls away from the bone. If roasting at home, cool, wrap and refrigerate birds then carry in cooler chest.
Serves 6

RUSSIAN REPAST

Instant Borsch (page 157) (In thermosware)
Piroshki* (Little Meat Turnovers)
Assorted Cheeses
Potato Salad (page 66)
Apples
Suggested wine: Johannisberg Riesling
or Gewürztraminer

*Recipes Follow

PIROSHKI

Filling

1 tablespoon butter
1/3 cup minced onion
1 small clove garlic, finely minced
2/3 cup minced fresh mushrooms
1/4 pound lean ground beef
1-1/2 teaspoons salt
fresh ground pepper to taste
2 teaspoons dill weed
2 tablespoons chopped parsley
white of 1 hard-boiled egg, finely minced
1 egg, beaten, for sealing
melted butter

Prepare white bread dough (page 25). Divide to form 2 loaves and set aside *half* for this recipe.

To prepare meat filling, melt butter in a skillet. Sauté chopped onion, garlic and mushrooms. Add the ground beef and cook until crumbly, breaking it up with a fork. Add seasonings and cook away most of the moisture. Put in a strainer to cool and to allow any excess juices or grease to drain off. Mix in minced egg white. Roll dough thinly on a lightly floured surface. Cut into 3-inch rounds. Place a teaspoon of filling in the center of each; fold over to form half-moon shapes. Brush edges with a bit of beaten egg to seal, then press and crimp edges together with fork tines. Place on a greased cookie sheet, cover and allow to rise until double in size. Brush with melted butter. Bake at 375° for 16 to 18 minutes or until brown. These can be made ahead and frozen; reheat before you leave or at picnic site. Carry wrapped in foil and several thicknesses of newspaper to keep warm for several hours. Also good cold.
Makes 16 rolls

EUROPEAN PICNIC

Chicken en Croûte*
String Bean Salad Bowl*
Tomato Wedges — Olives
Macaroni Salad (page 66)
Fresh Strawberries Tossed with Kirsch
Butter Cookies
Suggested wine: Sauvignon Blanc (dry or medium), Chardonnay or Pinot Blanc

*Recipes Follow

STRING BEAN SALAD BOWL

3 cups green beans, sliced diagonally
3 slices bacon, broiled crisp
4 cups mixed salad greens
2 green onions, chopped
2 hard-boiled eggs, shredded
French dressing (page 99)

Cook green beans until tender and still bright green. Crumble broiled bacon into bits. Tote salad greens in a plastic bag or a picnic container with a lid. Take other ingredients separately and toss together just before serving.
Serves 4 to 6

CHICKEN EN CROÛTE

3 whole chicken breasts, skinned and boned
1-1/2 cups chicken broth
1/2 cup sherry wine
6 thin slices ham
Dijon-style mustard
crushed, dried tarragon
6 thin slices Swiss cheese
6 frozen puff-pastry shells, defrosted

Poach the chicken breasts in chicken broth and sherry for 15 to 20 minutes or until tender. Cool and drain. (Save chicken stock for other uses.) Split chicken breasts in half lengthwise and wrap each piece in a thin slice of ham; coat it with a thin layer of Dijon-style mustard, sprinkle with tarragon and wrap in cheese.

Place thawed puff-pastry shells on a lightly floured surface and roll out each into a 4-inch circle. Wrap each chicken breast with a pastry circle. Wet edges with water, crimp and seal. Place on ungreased baking sheet. Bake at 400° for 20 minutes or until puffed and golden. Transfer to serving platter and cover with foil. Will stay warm for several hours. Serve warm or cold.
Serves 6

Nature is perfect, wherever we look,
but man always deforms it.
—J. C. F. Schiller: Die Braut von Messina, 1803

FONDUE PICNIC

Picnic Fondue*
Sourdough French Bread (page 19)
Artichokes* — Sliced Tomatoes
Baked Stuffed Peaches*
Cookies
Suggested wine: Pinot Chardonnay, Pinot Blanc, Traminer or Grey Riesling

*Recipes Follow

PICNIC FONDUE

1 clove garlic, split in half
3 tablespoons butter
3 tablespoons flour
1-1/3 cups dry white wine
3-1/2 cups shredded Emmentaler cheese
dash nutmeg
additional wine
1 loaf sourdough French bread

Rub the inside of the fondue cooker vigorously with the cut surface of the split garlic. Add butter and melt over moderate low heat. Remove from heat and blend in the flour. Gradually blend in the wine. Return saucepan to heat and warm until air bubbles come to the surface. Do not cover or allow to boil. Continue to stir at all times. Add a handful of the cheese. Wait until it has melted (keep stirring), then continue to add handfuls of the cheese, repeating this process. After all the cheese is combined and the fondue is bubbling *gently*, blend in the nutmeg and additional wine to keep proper dipping consistency. Each person spears a cube of bread with long-handled fondue forks and dips it into the pot. Add additional wine to thin mixture.

Fondue can be made at home or at the picnic site. To prepare it ahead of time, cool it thoroughly, then pour it into an insulated container or fondue pot. Refrigerate until ready to pack. Take along cut bread cubes in a plastic bag. Heat fondue in the pot over burning coals until hot and completely melted. Take along the extra wine to add if necessary.
Serves 6

ARTICHOKES

Select artichokes that are plump with tightly closed leaves. Overripe ones are hard-tipped with spreading leaves. With kitchen scissors snip off thorny tips of leaves. Cut stem end even at the bottom. Brush cut edges with lemon juice after trimming to prevent them from turning brown. Place the artichokes stem end down in a kettle of water which covers 1/3 of the vegetable. Add salt and 1 tablespoon lemon juice. Bring water to a boil and reduce to a simmer, cover and cook 40 to 45 minutes or until a leaf can be easily removed. Drain and cool. While warm, gently spread the top leaves and remove the fuzzy center choke. With a long-handled spoon carefully fill with mayonnaise, or mushrooms, shrimp or crab marinated in French dressing. Press leaves back up into original position. Chill. Take along in refrigerated cooler chest.

BAKED STUFFED PEACHES

3/4 cup macaroon cookie crumbs
1/3 cup finely ground toasted almonds
8 peaches
3 tablespoons sugar
1/3 to 1/2 cup Marsala wine

Dry macaroons in a slow oven. Crush with a rolling pin or break them up with a rotary beater or blender to form a medium consistency, not powdered. Combine the crumbs with the ground toasted almonds.

Select peaches that are ripe but firm. To skin dip them into boiling water. Cut in half and remove pit. With a serrated grapefruit spoon, scoop out some of the peach pulp to enlarge the center area and reserve peach pulp. Add sugar and 1/3 cup of the reserved peach pulp to the crumb and almond mixture. Divide filling into each peach half. Reassemble peach halves into a whole peach and secure with a toothpick. Place them in a shallow baking dish and sprinkle lightly with additional sugar. Pour the wine in the bottom of the dish. Cover and bake at 350° for 15 minutes or just until slightly tender. Cool them covered and then refrigerate. Serve chilled with wine sauce spooned over them. Take them along in the cooler chest.
Serves 8

GERMAN GRILL

Grilled Bratwurst*
Mustard — Horseradish — Dill Pickles
German Rye (page 30)
Potato Salad*
Sauerkraut Salad*
Orange Peel Cake*
Suggested beverage: Riesling, Green Hungarian, Lager, Ale or Beer

*Recipes Follow

BRATWURST

These are large German sausages of coarsely ground pork, frequently with veal, seasoned with salt, pepper, nutmeg, caraway, marjoram and often mace. They are plumper and lighter in color than the common frankfurters. Bratwurst sausages must not be eaten without first being cooked and are ideal for broiling or grilling. Keep refrigerated in cooler chest until cooking time. Grill 3 inches from the heat, about 5 minutes, taking care not to dry them out, keeping them as juicy as possible. If desired you can split them lengthwise, not quite all the way through, then broil or grill them cut side facing the heat, until just lightly browned. Allow 1 to 2 per serving.

SAUERKRAUT SALAD

1 27-ounce can sauerkraut
1/4 cup chopped green onions
1 cup shredded carrot
1/2 cup diced celery
1/2 cup chopped green pepper
2 tablespoons chopped pimiento

Dressing
1/2 cup sauerkraut juice
1/4 cup white wine vinegar
2/3 cup sugar

Drain the sauerkraut, saving 1/2 cup of the juice. In a large bowl combine the sauerkraut and other ingredients. Heat the reserved juice, wine vinegar and sugar in a saucepan until the sugar completely dissolves. Pour over the salad ingredients and mix. Spoon into picnic container and chill in refrigerator overnight. Keeps as long as 1 week.
Serves 6 to 8

POTATO SALAD GERMAN STYLE

2-1/2 pounds red-skinned potatoes
salt and pepper
1/2 cup white wine
dash garlic powder
4 to 5 green onions, chopped
2 tablespoons olive oil
2 tablespoons chopped parsley
3 tablespoons drained capers
2 tablespoons minced sweet-pickle relish
1 cup mayonnaise
2 hard-boiled eggs, sliced
1/2 sweet red pepper, minced
1/2 green pepper, minced
2 tablespoons crisp bacon bits

Boil the potatoes with skins on until just tender. While still warm, peel and slice into cubes or chunks. Sprinkle with salt and pepper. In a separate saucepan heat the wine until just warm (do not boil) with a dash of garlic powder. Pour over the warm potatoes which will absorb the wine. Toss gently. Sprinkle on the chopped green onions. Add olive oil, parsley, capers and sweet-pickle relish. Blend in enough mayonnaise to bind ingredients. Chill. At location or just before packing, garnish with egg slices, minced peppers and bacon.
For Box and Pail: Spoon into prechilled thermos.
At Cabin, in Galley or Camper: Can be served warm, or chilled.
For Picnics: Must be taken refrigerated.
Serves 8 to 10

ORANGE PEEL CAKE

1/4 pound softened butter
1 cup sugar
3 eggs
2 cups unbleached flour
1 teaspoon baking powder
1/2 teaspoon baking soda
1/4 teaspoon ground cardamom (optional)
2/3 cup buttermilk
1-1/2 to 2 tablespoons grated orange peel
1 cup chopped nuts

Topping
1/2 cup sugar
1/3 cup orange liqueur
1 cup orange juice

Making this a day ahead allows the cake to mellow; it keeps beautifully. Cream the butter and sugar together. Add the eggs, beating each one thoroughly. Sift the flour with the baking powder, soda and cardamom. Blend in the buttermilk alternately with the sifted ingredients. Fold in the grated orange peel and chopped nuts. Pour into a well-greased and floured 9-inch tube pan. Bake at 350° for 50 to 55 minutes. Combine the topping ingredients making sure the sugar is completely dissolved. While the cake is still hot, pierce the entire top with a long-tine fork or a skewer. *Slowly* pour the topping over the entire cake letting it all seep in. Leave cake in the pan overnight.
Serves 10 to 12

Setting out well is a quarter of the journey.
—H. G. Bohn: Handbook of Proverbs, 1855

MIDDLE EASTERN PICNIC

Avgolemono Soup (page 60) (In thermosware)
Arab Bread (page 37)
Lamb Filling with Mint Sauce*
Ripe Olives
Eggplant Salad*
Oranges with Marmalade Glaze*
Dates
Suggested wine: Zinfandel, Gamay

*Recipes Follow

EGGPLANT SALAD

1 medium eggplant (1 pound)
boiling salted water
2 to 3 green onions, sliced thin
1/2 cup chopped green pepper
3 medium tomatoes, peeled, seeded and diced
sprig parsley, chopped
1/4 cup white wine vinegar
1/3 cup lemon juice
1/2 cup olive or sesame oil
1 clove garlic, finely minced
1 teaspoon salt
1/2 teaspoon sugar
ground black pepper to taste
pomegranate seeds (optional)

Peel and cube the eggplant. Drop into boiling water and cook for 8 to 10 minutes, until barely tender but still firm. Drain and chill in the refrigerator. Toss eggplant with green onions, green pepper, diced tomatoes and chopped parsley. Several hours ahead of time, combine wine vinegar, lemon juice, oil, garlic, salt, sugar and pepper in a small jar. Shake dressing to blend thoroughly, pour over the salad ingredients and toss well to coat evenly. Turn into a plastic picnic container and refrigerate until ready to pack. Garnish with pomegranate seeds.
Serves 4 to 6

LAMB FILLING WITH MINT SAUCE

2 large onions, sliced very thin
olive oil
2 pounds ground lamb
2 cloves garlic, mashed and minced
1/4 teaspoon whole coriander seed (optional)
1/2 teaspoon cumin
1/8 teaspoon powdered cloves
1/2 teaspoon cinnamon
1 teaspoon salt
pepper to taste
1/2 cup chopped pine nuts

Sauté the sliced onions in olive oil; drain and set aside. Brown the lamb until all redness is gone and meat is crumbly. Pour off excess grease. Add sautéed onions, minced garlic and seasonings. Cook 25 to 30 minutes. Cool thoroughly. Turn into a container, cover and refrigerate. Sauté pine nuts separately in a small amount of olive oil until lightly golden. Drain, cool and place in a small covered container.
At Picnic Site: Reheat meat filling on hibachi or campfire and spoon into the pocket of each round of Arab bread; sprinkle on the sautéed pine nuts and dribble on some mint sauce.

Mint Sauce
1-1/2 cups chopped fresh mint leaves, no stems
1/2 cup wine or malt vinegar
1/4 cup water
1/4 cup sugar

Wash mint leaves and pat dry on paper towels. When thoroughly dry, chop. Heat vinegar, water and sugar together. Pour over the leaves and allow to stand for several hours. Pour into a small jar or container. Use hot or cold.
Makes about 1-1/2 cups sauce

ORANGES WITH MARMALADE GLAZE

Prepare 2 to 3 large oranges by removing all the rind, membranes and the white pith. Cut them in half lengthwise, then slice thin, and arrange slices overlapping in a flat, square container. Sprinkle with curaçao or any orange-flavored liqueur.
Glaze: Melt 1/3 cup of orange marmalade; stir in 3 to 4 tablespoons liqueur. Pour over the sliced oranges. Cover and chill until serving time.
Serves 4 to 6

GREEK PICNIC

Tyropokita* (Greek Feta Cheese Turnovers)
Sliced Tomatoes Garnished with Anchovies and Ripe Olives
Marinated Artichoke Hearts
Mediterranean Lemon Cake*
Suggested wine: Pinot Blanc, Johannisberg Riesling or Traminer

*Recipes Follow

TYROPOKITA

6 frozen puff-pastry shells
3/4 to 1 pound feta cheese, crumbled
3 tablespoons fresh lemon juice
3 tablespoons minced onion
1 clove garlic, very finely minced
3 tablespoons chopped fresh mint
(or 1 teaspoon dried)
1 teaspoon dried oregano
1 cup finely chopped fresh spinach leaves
1/2 cup chopped parsley
2 egg yolks, room temperature
2 egg whites, room temperature
1/4 teaspoon ground pepper
cinnamon

Defrost the frozen pastry shells at room temperature for 1 hour or until soft enough to roll out. In a large bowl combine the feta cheese, lemon juice, minced onion, garlic, chopped mint, oregano, chopped spinach and parsley. Blend in the beaten egg *yolks*. Mix thoroughly.

Then on a lightly floured surface roll out the defrosted pastry shells into 7-inch circles. On each half pastry circle put several tablespoons of the cheese filling and sprinkle lightly with cinnamon. Lightly beat egg whites, brush around the outer edge of the pastry and fold over. With a fork press around the edges to seal in the filling. Brush the tops with egg white. Place on ungreased cookie sheet and bake at 375° for 20 to 25 minutes or until puffed and golden. Can be served hot or cold. *For Picnics:* Bake *just* before leaving. While hot transfer to a serving dish. Pack in single layer; cover with foil. Will stay warm for several hours.
Makes 6

MEDITERRANEAN LEMON CAKE

1/2 pound softened butter
1-1/2 cups sugar
4 eggs, room temperature
1 tablespoon grated lemon peel
2-1/2 cups unbleached flour
1/2 teaspoon salt
1 teaspoon baking soda
1 teaspoon baking powder
1/2 pint yogurt, room temperature
3/4 cup finely ground nuts
1/2 cup lemon juice

Cream the softened butter and 1 cup of the sugar together until light and fluffy. Add eggs and the lemon peel; blend thoroughly. Sift the flour, salt, baking soda and baking powder together. Add dry ingredients alternately with the yogurt. Fold in the ground nuts. Turn into a well-greased 9-inch tube pan. Bake at 350° for 1 hour or until a toothpick inserted in the top comes out clean. Combine the 1/2 cup sugar and lemon juice in a saucepan. Heat until sugar has dissolved and pour over the cake while still warm. Allow cake to cool in the pan.
Serves 6 to 8

Give us the luxuries of life,
and we will dispense with its necessaries.
—O. W. Holmes:
The Autocrat of the Breakfast-Table, VI, 1858

MEDITERRANEAN PICNIC

Lamb Shish Kabob*
Arab Bread (page 37)
Feli's Chumus* (Arabic Appetizer)
Olives and Pickled Pepperoncini
Cucumber and Radish Salad*
Kataifi*
Suggested wine: Zinfandel or Gamay

*Recipes Follow

CUCUMBER AND RADISH SALAD

2/3 cup white wine vinegar
2 teaspoons salt
2 tablespoons sugar
1/4 teaspoon ground black pepper
sprig parsley, chopped
1 bunch radishes, thinly sliced
3 medium cucumbers, peeled and thinly sliced
salt

Combine vinegar, salt, sugar and black pepper to make a dressing. Sprinkle radish and cucumber slices with salt and allow to stand for 1 to 2 hours. Pour off all the accumulated liquids. Place in a covered container, add chopped parsley and pour on dressing. Marinate in refrigerator overnight.
Serves 6

FELI'S CHUMUS

2 cups cooked garbanzo or ceci beans
1 cup reserved bean liquid
1 cup sesame tahini*
juice of 1 lemon
2 to 3 cloves garlic
1 to 1-1/2 teaspoons salt
olive oil
chopped parsley

Purée the cooked garbanzo beans with a rotary beater or in an electric blender until smooth, gradually adding the reserved bean liquid. Add the sesame tahini, lemon juice, garlic and salt to taste. Whirl once again until a smooth, thick purée. Spoon out into a traveling container with a lid and chill. To serve authentically, dribble the chumus with olive oil, garnish with chopped parsley, olives and pepperoncini. Each person tears his Arab bread into bite-size pieces and scoops up the chumus.
Serves 6

*Sesame tahini is ground hulled sesame-seed paste that can be purchased in health-food stores. Keep refrigerated once opened; will keep for many months. When first opened carefully stir in the oil that rises to the surface.

LAMB SHISH KABOB

3 pounds lean lamb
2 tablespoons red wine vinegar
1/3 cup lemon juice
1/3 cup olive oil
1 to 2 cloves garlic, crushed
12 large mushrooms
2 medium-sized green peppers,
seeded and quartered
12 cherry tomatoes
3 small white onions, peeled and quartered

Cut lamb into 1-1/2- to 2-inch cubes, removing any gristle and fat. Combine the wine vinegar, lemon juice, olive oil and garlic. Pour over the lamb and marinate covered for 12 hours. Drain, wrap and pack in cooler chest along with mushrooms, peppers, tomatoes and onions. Once there, thread meat on 6 12-inch skewers alternating the lamb with other ingredients. Grill 20 to 25 minutes about 5 inches from the hot coals, turning and basting with the extra marinade. Or thread the skewers at home, wrap them in foil and tote in the cooler chest.
Serves 6

KATAIFI

12 shredded-wheat biscuits
1-1/2 cups hot milk
2 tablespoons sugar
1/2 pound butter, melted
1/4 cup shelled and chopped pistachio nuts
2 cups coarsely ground walnuts

Syrup
1/4 cup sugar
1/4 cup water
1/2 cup honey
1 teaspoon lemon or orange juice

Kataifi pastry is like shredded wheat, but soft. Buy it at Near Eastern shops or substitute shredded wheat.

Dip each shredded-wheat biscuit, one at a time, in hot milk until thoroughly saturated; drain briefly. Cut each one in half lengthwise. Lay half the biscuit halves in a 9x10-inch square shallow baking pan. Sprinkle with 2 tablespoons of sugar, pour on half the melted butter and top with the chopped nuts. Cover with the rest of the biscuits, putting them back together. Pour on the rest of the melted butter, let it soak in, then *press down firmly.* Bake at 350° for 30 minutes or until lightly browned. Prepare syrup by heating sugar, water and honey in a saucepan until sugar is dissolved. Remove from heat and stir in the lemon or orange juice. Pour over biscuits while hot. Cover and cool 2 hours before packing. Cut in 2-inch squares.
Serves 6 to 8

SKEWERED SUPPER

Chicken and Beef Kabobs*
Herb-Seasoned Picnic Loaf (page 33)
Assorted Cheeses
Columbine Salad*
Melt-Away Butter Cakes*
Season's Fresh Fruit
Suggested wine: Cabernet Sauvignon, Zinfandel

*Recipes Follow

CHICKEN AND BEEF KABOBS

1-1/2 pounds New York or filet steak
2 whole chicken breasts, skinned
3/4 cup burgundy wine
2 tablespoons lemon juice
1/3 cup olive oil
1 clove garlic, mashed
1 small onion, thinly sliced
2 tablespoons soy sauce
2 tablespoons sugar
grinding black pepper

Cut beef into 1-1/2-inch cubes and the chicken into 1-inch cubes. (The larger beef cubes should be slightly rare, while the smaller chicken cubes should be thoroughly cooked.) Combine remaining ingredients in a jar and shake well. Pour this mixture over cubed meats in a large glass bowl and marinate in refrigerator overnight. Drain thoroughly and wrap for packing. Tote in the cooler chest. At picnic site thread cubed meat and chicken alternately on skewers; barbecue over hot coals, approximately 3 inches from the heat. Cook 3 to 4 minutes, turning and basting often.
Serves 6 to 8

COLUMBINE SALAD

1 head escarole lettuce
2 cups cubed casaba or cantaloupe melon
2 tender inside celery stalks, sliced
2 tablespoons chopped pimiento
French dressing (page 99)

Wash and dry lettuce leaves; tear into pieces. Take lettuce in a plastic bag or container with a lid. Carry other ingredients separately. Just before serving toss ingredients together.
Serves 4 to 6

MELT-AWAY BUTTER CAKES

1/2 pound softened butter
1-1/2 cups sugar
1 egg, beaten
1/4 teaspoon salt
1 teaspoon grated lemon rind
1 teaspoon pure lemon extract
2-1/2 cups sifted unbleached white flour

Cream the softened butter with the sugar. Add all but 1 tablespoon of the egg, salt, lemon rind and extract. Work in the sifted flour a few tablespoons at a time until thoroughly blended. Turn dough out onto a lightly floured surface and knead for just a few minutes. Pat dough out flat in a 8-inch round greased baking pan. Brush with reserved tablespoon of beaten egg. Bake at 350° for 40 to 45 minutes or until golden. Allow cake to cool 30 minutes. Remove from pan and cut into serving pieces. Cake will harden as it cools. Store in airtight container. Keeps well for a long time. It is the perfect cake to go with a macédoine (page 101).
Variation: In place of lemon rind and extract, use 1/2 teaspoon ground ginger and 2 tablespoons minced crystalized ginger.
Serves 6

How hard it is to hide the sparks of nature!
—Shakespeare: Cymbeline, 1609

AMERICAN BARBECUE

Barbecue Spareribs*
Cheese Bread (page 29)
Corn on the Coals*
Asparagus Salad*
Tarragon Carrots*
Watermel-Rum*
Cookies
Suggested wine: Gamay or Gamay Beaujolais

*Recipes Follow

CORN ON THE COALS

Allow 1 to 2 ears of fresh sweet corn per person. Strip and pull husks down to the end of the cob, but do not remove. Discard the corn *silk* only. Brush with garlic butter. Pull husks up into original place around the corn, making sure all the kernels are covered. Encase each ear of corn in double thickness of heavy-duty aluminum foil, twisting the ends to seal completely. Roast the corn among the hot coals, turning several times for even cooking, approximately 20 to 25 minutes.

In place of foil, tie ends of husks closed with small pieces of fine wire at the tip of the cob. Place corn in husks on the grill. Dip a clean burlap sack in water and wring it out. Place it over the corn and let it steam. For this method allow 8 to 10 minutes for *each* side.

BARBECUE SPARERIBS

1 8-ounce can tomato sauce
1 cup orange or pineapple juice
2 tablespoons brown sugar
1 tablespoon cider vinegar
1/2 teaspoon Worcestershire sauce
1/2 teaspoon chili powder
4 drops liquid smoke
1 teaspoon soy sauce or salt
2-1/2 to 3-1/2 pounds spareribs

Combine the sauce ingredients in order given. Place in a container with a tight-fitting lid. Take in cooler chest. Select lean meaty pork or lamb spareribs. Allow 1/2 pound per person. Have the butcher crack ribs for easier serving, but leave in one piece. Salt and pepper ribs. Wrap in foil and take in cooler chest. If you wish to reduce cooking time, precook the ribs at home in a 350° oven until just barely tender. Cool, wrap in foil and then complete the cooking with the basting sauce at the picnic site. Spareribs can also be cooked in a revolving basket on a barbecue spit.

Barbecue spareribs 4 to 5 inches from hot briquettes, turning them several times so the ribs will not dry out, grilling them for 30 to 40 minutes. Then brush with prepared barbecue sauce, grilling an additional 15 to 20 minutes or until cooked to the desired doneness.
Serves 4

ASPARAGUS SALAD

2 pounds fresh asparagus
vinaigrette dressing (page 99)
1 hard-boiled egg, shredded
pimiento for garnish (optional)

Wash and trim asparagus, snapping off tough ends and removing scales, if sandy. Cook in 1 inch of boiling salted water for 8 to 10 minutes. Do not overcook. Asparagus must be green and a bit firm-to-the-tooth. Asparagus stalks can also be cooked standing upright in a narrow, deep pot or a coffee pot, 10 to 12 minutes. Drain thoroughly. Lay asparagus in a flat, square container with a lid. Pour on the dressing, cover and chill. Shred the hard-boiled egg into a separate container. Take along and just before serving garnish the asparagus with shredded egg and strips of pimiento.
Serves 6

TARRAGON CARROTS

2 pounds small baby carrots
3/4 cup white tarragon vinegar
2 tablespoons sugar
1/2 teaspoon salt
grinding of black pepper to taste
1 teaspoon dried tarragon
2 tablespoons chopped parsley
2 tablespoons chopped green onion

Scrape and clean carrots; leave whole or cut into desired lengths. Drop carrots into boiling water and cook until just tender, about 8 minutes, and drain. Meanwhile combine the rest of the ingredients and pour over the cooked carrots while still warm. Cover and refrigerate overnight. Drain and pack in traveling container with a tight-fitting lid.
Serves 6

WATERMEL-RUM

Cut out a deep, 2-inch-square plug on the top side of a medium-to-large ripe watermelon. Slowly pour light rum into the watermelon, a small amount at a time until the melon can absorb no more. Replace the plug, sealing it with heavy tape. Chill for at least 8 hours. Slice to serve.

MEXICAN PICNIC

Sangría* (In thermosware)
Tortas* (Mexican-Style Sandwich)
Aztec Spread* (Guacamole)
Macaroni Salad Con Chicos*
Season's Fresh Melon

*Recipes Follow

AZTEC SPREAD (GUACAMOLE)

2 ripe avocados, peeled and pitted
juice of 1/2 lemon
1 tablespoon grated onion
dash Tabasco sauce

Mash avocados with a fork, blending in the lemon juice until smooth and creamy. Add the onion and Tabasco to taste. Put in a container with a tight-fitting lid and chill. Take in cooler chest. Or if desired, prepare at picnic site just before serving.
Makes approximately 1-3/4 cups

SANGRÍA

1/3 cup lemon juice
1/2 cup orange juice
1/3 cup powdered sugar or very fine sugar
1 bottle (4/5 quart) burgundy
1/4 cup brandy
1/4 cup Cointreau
1 orange sliced thin
1 lime sliced thin
1 7-ounce bottle club soda

Combine fruit juices and sugar in a large glass pitcher and stir until sugar is completely dissolved. Add wine, brandy and Cointreau and the sliced fruits. Chill at least 2 to 3 hours or even overnight. Tote in a 1/2-gallon thermos jug and add the club soda just before serving. White sangría is made the same way but substitute a chablis, Chenin Blanc or Rhine wine for the burgundy.
Serves 8 to 10

MACARONI SALAD CON CHICOS
(Southwestern Flavor)

2 cups cooked, cooled macaroni
  (1 cup uncooked)
1/4 cup chopped olives
2 hard-boiled eggs, chopped
1 cup shredded cheddar cheese
2 chopped green onions
2 tablespoons chopped parsley
1/2 cup chopped celery
dash Tabasco sauce
  (or 1/4 cup minced green chilies to taste)
3/4 to 1 cup mayonnaise
tomato wedges for garnish

Combine all the ingredients in order given blending thoroughly. Put in picnic container with a lid and refrigerate until packing time. Tote in the cooler chest. Garnish with tomato slices at serving time.
Serves 6

TORTAS

1 flank steak
juice of 1 lemon or 1 orange
1/3 cup vegetable oil
1 clove garlic, finely minced
2 tablespoons grated onion
1/2 teaspoon bottled salsa (jalapeña sauce)
6 French rolls or tortillas
Aztec spread (preceding recipe)
Monterey Jack cheese, thinly sliced
shredded lettuce

Score the flank steak in diagonal slashes on both sides and place in a flat glass container. Combine the lemon or orange juice with oil, garlic, onion and salsa; pour over meat and marinate at least 4 hours. Drain, wrap in foil and pack in cooler chest. Broil or grill 3 to 4 minutes on each side or as desired. Carve meat diagonally into thin slices. This can also be served cold: broiled at home, taken in cooler chest and sliced just before serving.

Lay strips of steak on French roll or tortillas. Spread with mayonnaise if desired and top with guacamole, cheese slices and shredded lettuce. If you wish to heat tortillas, place them directly on the grill and flip once until tortillas are hot, about 1 minute each side. Stack and keep warm off to the side in foil or wrapped in dampened cloth or heat them as needed for each serving.
Serves 6

SOUTH OF THE BORDER

Gazpacho* (In thermosware)
Barbecued Steaks with Salsa Jalapeña
Bolillos (page 42)
Ensalada Atún*
Assorted Fresh Fruit
Pecan Toscas* (Little Cakes)
Suggested wine: Cabernet Sauvignon, Barbera

*Recipes Follow

GAZPACHO

1 cucumber, peeled and chopped
1 onion, chopped
1 clove garlic, minced very fine
1 green pepper, seeded and chopped
1 tomato, peeled and chopped
1/2 teaspoon crushed oregano
pinch cumin (optional)
1 teaspoon salt
dash Tabasco
2 tablespoons white wine vinegar
1 tablespoon lemon juice
3 tablespoons olive oil
4 cups tomato juice
1 ripe avocado
2 green onions, chopped

Combine all ingredients except avocado and green onions. Chill thoroughly. Pour into thermosware just before leaving. Take avocado and chopped green onions along separately. To serve pour gazpacho into mugs and top with avocado slices and chopped onions.
Serves 6

ENSALADA ATÚN

6 to 8 cups mixed salad greens, torn
1 6-ounce can white tuna
6 to 8 pimiento-stuffed green olives, sliced
1/4 cup chopped parsley
1 red onion, sliced paper thin

Dressing
2 teaspoons salt
1/4 teaspoon ground black pepper
5 tablespoons white wine vinegar
1/4 teaspoon Dijon-style mustard
1/4 teaspoon dry tarragon
3/4 cup olive oil

Tote washed and dried greens in a plastic bag or picnic container with a lid. Drain tuna and flake it into a separate covered container. Place other ingredients in another container or plastic wrap. Combine dressing ingredients in a jar. Assemble and toss salad just before eating.
Serves 6

PECAN TOSCAS
(Little Cakes)

1-1/2 cubes softened butter
2 cups unbleached flour
1/2 cup sugar

Blend ingredients with rotary beater or a pastry blender until crumbly. Divide into 12 small muffin tins. Press and hollow the centers by pushing dough up and around the sides to form a small tart shell. Bake at 350° for 8 to 10 minutes.

Filling
1 cup finely chopped pecans
1/2 cup sugar
4 teaspoons flour
4 tablespoons butter
4 to 5 tablespoons cream
1 teaspoon vanilla extract

Combine ingredients in a small saucepan. Cook over moderate heat and bring to the boiling point, stirring constantly. Quickly spoon into the warm tart shells and return to the oven for another 8 minutes. Cool for 10 minutes and then carefully remove them from the tins.
Makes 12 tarts

Those things are better which are perfected by nature than those which are finished by art.
—Cicero: De natura deorum II, 45 B.C.

SOUTH SEAS LUAU

Ono Ono Wai (Spiked Iced Tea)*
Tahitian Chicken* — Cardamom Buns(page 44)
Island Salad*
Coconut Upside-Down Cake*
Suggested wine: Rosé or Semillon, instead of spiked iced tea

*Recipes Follow

ONO ONO WAI (SPIKED ICED TEA)

1/3 cup lemon juice
1/2 cup sugar
4 cups strong iced tea
1-1/2 cups dark rum
lemon slices

Add the lemon and sugar to the tea when first prepared and still hot, stirring until the sugar is completely dissolved. Blend in the rum. Chill. Pour into prechilled thermosware just before leaving. Garnish glasses with lemon slices.
Serves 4 to 6

ISLAND SALAD

4 cups mixed salad greens
1 dozen medium prawns, cooked
French dressing (page 99)
2 to 3 papayas

Tote washed and dried salad greens in a plastic bag. Marinate cooked prawns in French dressing. Carry all ingredients in cooler chest. At picnic site peel, seed and slice the papayas into quarters. (Plan on 1/4 wedge for each person.) Arrange on salad greens and garnish with marinated prawns.
Serves 4 to 6

TAHITIAN CHICKEN

3 whole chicken breasts, split in half and boned
1/3 cup tarragon vinegar
1/2 cup pineapple juice
1/3 cup sesame oil
1 teaspoon powdered ginger
1 tablespoon soy sauce
1/2 cup honey
preserved kumquats
1 fresh pineapple, sliced

Place chicken breasts in a shallow 1-1/2-quart glass dish. Combine vinegar, pineapple juice, oil, ginger, soy sauce and honey in a jar. Shake well and pour over the chicken. Marinate for several hours, turning pieces several times. Drain and save marinade. Transfer chicken to a plastic traveling container or wrap in foil. Take reserved marinade along separately for basting. Grill chicken breasts over hot coals basting often. Serve with kumquats and pineapple slices.

To prepare pineapple, cut off peel, slice and cut out core. Place slices in a picnic container with a lid. Chill until packing time.
Serves 4 to 6

COCONUT UPSIDE-DOWN CAKE

5 tablespoons butter, melted
1/2 cup brown sugar, firmly packed
1 cup grated coconut
1/4 cup sliced almonds
4 tablespoons shortening
2/3 cup sugar
1 egg
1 cup sifted cake flour
1-1/2 teaspoons baking powder
1/4 teaspoon salt
1/3 cup milk
1 teaspoon vanilla extract

Melt the butter and pour into a 9-inch cake pan. Crumble on the brown sugar and sprinkle with coconut and sliced almonds.

To prepare cake batter, cream the shortening and sugar together until smooth. Add the egg and beat well. Sift dry ingredients together and add alternately to sugar-egg mixture with the milk. Blend in the vanilla. Pour batter carefully over the topping, spreading evenly. Bake 350° for 30 to 35 minutes. Invert onto serving dish immediately and allow to rest 3 to 4 minutes before gently lifting off the cake pan.
Serves 6

CHINESE PICNIC

Iced Tea (In thermosware)
Cantonese Chicken Kabobs*
Ginger Biscuits (page 45)
Chinese Cabbage and Carrot Coleslaw*
Chinese Almond Cookies*

*Recipes Follow

CHINESE CABBAGE AND CARROT COLESLAW

1 small Chinese white cabbage (1 to 1-1/2 pounds)
2 medium carrots, peeled and shredded
3 green onions, chopped
2 cups bean sprouts
1 teaspoon salt
ground black pepper to taste
2 tablespoons chopped parsley
2 tablespoons sugar
3 tablespoons French dressing
3/4 to 1 cup mayonnaise

Remove outer leaves of cabbage and center core. Cut in half lengthwise and shred very thin. Combine with other ingredients, toss and mix well. Cover and refrigerate until packing time. Tote in cooler chest. Toss once again before serving.
Serves 6

CANTONESE CHICKEN KABOBS

3 whole chicken breasts, skinned and boned
3/4 cup dry sherry wine
2 tablespoons sesame oil
2 tablespoons soy sauce
1/2 teaspoon sugar
4 to 5 slices fresh ginger root
1 clove garlic, minced
pineapple chunks
green pepper chunks
quartered onions
cherry tomatoes
mushrooms

Cut chicken breasts into 1-inch pieces. Combine in a large bowl with sherry, oil, soy sauce, sugar, ginger and garlic; marinate overnight. Drain and reserve the marinade. Wrap chicken in foil and pack in cooler chest. Just before cooking, loosely thread pieces on skewers so they are just touching. On separate skewers alternate pineapple chunks, onions, green pepper, cherry tomatoes, mushrooms or any combination of vegetables you desire. Brush with sesame oil or some of the reserved marinade. Broil or grill chicken and vegetable kabobs, basting with marinade. Cook 15 to 20 minutes or until chicken is golden. Add vegetable kabobs during the last 5 to 10 minutes. If using a barbecue rack, broil about 4 inches from the hot coals. Turn frequently for even cooking and baste often.
Serves 6

CHINESE ALMOND COOKIES

2-1/2 cups sifted unbleached flour
1/2 cup ground blanched almonds
1-1/2 teaspoons baking powder
pinch salt
1-1/2 cubes softened butter
2 teaspoons pure almond extract
1/2 cup sugar
2 egg yolks
whole blanched almonds for garnish

In a large bowl combine all ingredients except the egg yolks and the whole almonds. Knead dough until smooth. Break off pieces and form into approximately 20 balls. Flatten into small, round cakes. Place on ungreased cookie sheets 2 inches apart. Beat egg yolks with 1 tablespoon of water; brush on cookies and press a whole almond onto the top. Bake at 375° for 10 to 12 minutes.
Makes about 20 cookies

He that follows nature is never out of his way.
—T. Fuller, 1732

PATHFINDER'S KNAPSACK

Any veteran backpacker knows that streamlined planning is essential to a successful outing. However, the enthusiastic novice should be cautious, acquiring equipment gradually and learning by experience. Too often, equipment is bought compulsively and later found useless. By planning you will save time and money.

This particular chapter is designed to enlarge the menu selection for old-timers and give suggestions to newcomers. In addition, the food lists will be helpful in determining weight and bulk.

Most professional climbers assemble their own packs, maintaining lightweight, easily prepared foods, organized by the day. These food packets are bundled and labeled. Although there are many freeze-dried, dehydrated, prepackaged foods available from camping suppliers, they are expensive and often skimpy. They hardly accommodate an outdoor appetite. As an alternative compile your own selection of foods from conventional foodstore items.

Very few, if any backpackers carry a recipe book. Therefore, emphasis is on simplicity and nutrition. There are a number of semi-perishable, high-protein foods that can be carried for the first few days, such as dry salami, bacon and cheese. However, nonperishable food is a better choice, possibly supplemented with fish or foraged foods.

Good food makes for good traveling companions. Dispositions remain on the bright side when the stomach is full. Because hiking requires a tremendous consumption of energy, be sure the nutritional value of the food is high. Ideally, high-energy foods—bacon, oils, cream, butter and nuts—meet these needs. But, since it is difficult to digest fats at high altitudes, a carbohydrate diet of rice, bread, cereals, crackers, dried fruits and potatoes is practical. For snacking enjoy a pocketful of grop (gorp), granola or cookies filled with nuts, raisins and dried fruits. For additional protein try beef jerky, nuts, peanut butter, cheese, dried meats, powdered milk and eggs. Canned meats, with extra weight taken into consideration, might include corned beef, chicken, tuna or Canadian bacon. To stay healthy, sustain your daily diet with some form of vitamin C, in fresh or tablet form. To increase protein value, add dry skim milk to mixed or cooked foods.

When hiking, preserve the wilderness. Take your refuse back with you or to designated dumping areas. Wild animals smell the odors of foods left on buried cans or wrappers. If you cannot burn your refuse and it is not biodegradable, save one knapsack pocket, lined with a plastic bag so that you can stow and condense your wrappers, press and stamp cans and return it all for proper disposal and recycling. Pack to preserve our environment for the enjoyment of others.

SEMI-PERISHABLES
(Can travel for the first few days)

Slab bacon
Dry salami
Cheeses: natural Swiss, cheddar, Stilton
Hydrogenated vegetable shortening
(in a small plastic container)
Vegetable oil (in a plastic bottle)

UNPERISHABLES, LIMITED WEIGHT

Canned meats: Canadian bacon,
corned beef, boned chicken
Canned seafood: oysters, clams,
salmon, sardines, etc.

UNPERISHABLES, LIGHTWEIGHT

Bouillon cubes: beef and chicken
Biscuit mix
Cereals: oatmeal, cream of wheat, etc.
Dried fruits: raisins, apricots, figs, prunes, pears
Dried vegetables for seasoning: dehydrated
green pepper, onion, toasted onions
Dried mushrooms
Popcorn kernels
Seasoned croutons
Crackers: soda, graham, etc.
Marshmallows
Chocolate bars
Condiments: catsup, mustard, jams or
jellies (in plastic containers)
Relishes: pickles and pepperoncini (can travel due to
the brine and vinegar; tote in plastic containers)
Herbs and spices (in individual plastic packets;
make up your own blends, page 151.)
Seasoning salts (instead of carrying several
different kinds of spices)
Nuts: all kinds (excellent source of protein)
Peanut butter (packed in a plastic container)
Powdered eggs (two eggs are equivalent to
a serving of meat, excellent source of iron)
Powdered skim milk (inexpensive source of
protein and calcium)
Breads: Mexican corn or flour tortillas,
Arab bread (page 37)
Coffee: fresh ground or instant
Tea
Dried beans, peas, lentils (other excellent sources
of protein for a main dish; inexpensive, *but
will require a long time of cooking)*
Pasta
Rice
Dehydrated potatoes (enrich with powdered
skim milk when preparing)

BEEF JERKY # 1

2-1/2 pounds flank steak
1/2 cup soy sauce
1/4 teaspoon garlic powder
ground black pepper to taste

Trim off *all* visible fat. (Jerky keeps indefinitely if all fat is removed.) Cut the flank steak lengthwise with the grain in long, *thin* strips. Combine the soy sauce, garlic and pepper. Pour over the beef strips and marinate for 1 hour. Place on wire rack over a baking sheet. Arrange strips so that they *do not* overlap. Bake at 150° to 175°, 10 to 12 hours. Store in an airtight container.

BEEF JERKY # 2

3 pounds round steak
hickory smoke salt
1/4 teaspoon garlic powder
ground black pepper to taste
sugar

Trim off all visible fat. (Jerky keeps indefinitely if all fat is removed.) Cut the meat lengthwise into long, thin strips. Place meat strips in a flat dish. Sprinkle each layer generously with seasonings; let stand about 4 hours. Place meat on wire racks over a baking sheet; do not overlap. Place in a cool oven; turn heat to 150° to 200°; bake 12 to 16 hours, depending upon the thickness of the meat.

GROP

Grop or gorp, as it is sometimes called, is a high-energy snack. I prefer grop because when hiking or bike riding, a person naturally gropes for the item in his pack.

BASIC GROP

1 cup raisins
1 cup candied chocolate bits or carob
1 cup salted peanuts

Combine ingredients and divide into individual packets. Store in airtight container.

GOURMET GROP

1 cup dark seedless raisins
1 cup white raisins
1 cup unblanched almonds
1 cup diced dried apricots
1 cup candied chocolate bits or carob
1 cup macadamia nuts
1 cup walnuts
1 cup cashew nuts

Combine all ingredients and divide into individual packets. Store in airtight containers.

BOMBAY GROP

1/4 cup uncooked lentils
1/4 cup long-grain rice
1/4 cup split peas
3 cups water
3 tablespoons oil
2 tablespoons sesame seeds
1/2 teaspoon ground coriander
1/2 teaspoon ground cumin
1/4 teaspoon turmeric (optional)
1 cup roasted salted peanuts
1 cup salted cashews
1/4 cup dark seedless raisins
a wee pinch cayenne pepper
1/4 teaspoon ground cloves
1/2 teaspoon salt

Wash the lentils, rice and split peas. Turn into 3 cups boiling water for 1 to 2 minutes. Remove from heat; cover and allow to steep for 10 minutes. Drain thoroughly; rinse with cold water and spread out on paper towels to dry.

In a skillet heat the oil over moderate heat. Sauté the lentils, rice, peas and sesame seeds. Stir and blend in coriander, cumin and turmeric. Continue to sauté for 10 to 15 minutes. Take off the heat and blend in the nuts, raisins, cayenne, cloves and salt. Store in an airtight container. Keeps for a week or longer.
Makes approximately 3 cups

BREAKFAST-IN-A-COOKIE

1/3 cup whole bran cereal
1/4 cup orange juice
1-1/2 cubes softened butter or margarine
1/4 cup sugar
1 egg
1/4 cup honey
1-1/2 teaspoons vanilla extract
1 cup white unbleached flour, unsifted
1 teaspoon baking powder
1/2 teaspoon baking soda
1/2 teaspoon salt
1/3 cup nonfat dry milk
2 teaspoons grated orange rind
1 cup regular or quick-cooking oatmeal
1 cup finely chopped walnuts or your choice
1 cup raisins

In a small bowl, combine the bran and orange juice and set aside. In another bowl cream the butter and sugar together. Add the egg and beat until light. Blend in the honey, vanilla and the bran-orange mixture. Combine together the flour, baking powder, baking soda, salt, dry milk, orange rind, oatmeal, nuts and raisins. Stir dry mixture into the creamed mixture. Drop by level tablespoons onto greased cookie sheets, about 2 inches apart. Bake at 375° for 10 to 12 minutes or until golden brown.
Makes 3-1/2 to 4 dozen cookies

Nature will always maintain her rights,
and prevail in the end
over any abstract reasoning whatsoever.
—David Hume: Essays Moral and Political, I, 1741

GRANOLA CEREAL

1/4 cup vegetable oil
1/3 cup honey
2 cups rolled oats
1/2 cup raisins
1/3 cup wheat germ
1/4 cup slivered almonds
3 tablespoons sesame seeds
1 cup shredded coconut

Combine all ingredients in a large mixing bowl, increasing amount of nuts if you wish. Spread ingredients out in a shallow pan and allow to set 10 to 12 minutes in a 350° oven to dry. If desired, toast the granola under the broiler, but watch carefully. Store in an airtight container.

IRENE'S GRANOLA

1/2 cup brown sugar
1/4 cup water
3 tablespoons butter
1 teaspoon vanilla
3 cups old-fashioned rolled oats
1/4 cup wheat germ
1/4 cup coconut
1/4 cup slivered almonds
1/4 cup sesame seeds

Combine all ingredients and spread out on a shallow ungreased cookie sheet or a jelly-roll type of pan. Toast in a 350° oven 15 to 20 minutes, stirring frequently, until ingredients are brown. Store in an airtight container.

JORIOLA

1 cup rolled oats
1 cup wheat flakes or bran
1/2 cup wheat germ
1/2 cup pumpkin seeds
1/2 cup sesame seeds
1/2 cup sunflower seeds
1/4 cup honey
1/4 cup vegetable oil
1/4 cup hot water
assorted dried fruits
cinnamon
salt

Combine all ingredients except dried fruits, cinnamon and salt and spread out on a shallow, ungreased cookie sheet or a jelly-roll type of pan. Over the top sprinkle your choice of assorted diced dried fruits—raisins, currants, dates, prunes, pears, apricots—whatever you prefer. Now sprinkle lightly with cinnamon and possibly a pinch of salt. Toast in a 250° oven for 1/2 hour stirring frequently. Store in an airtight container. (This recipe was inspired by Alice Peterson of Santa Cruz.)

NATURE'S NIBBLES

1/2 pound softened butter
2 cups brown sugar, firmly packed
2 eggs
2 teaspoons grated orange or lemon rind
3 tablespoons orange or lemon juice
2 cups white unbleached flour
1 teaspoon salt
1 teaspoon baking soda
2-1/2 cups rolled oats
1/2 cup coconut
1-1/2 cups diced dates
1 cup finely chopped mixed nuts (almonds, pecans, peanuts, your choice)

Cream softened butter and brown sugar together. Blend in the eggs, orange or lemon rind and juice. In another bowl combine the flour, salt, baking soda, oats and coconut. Stir into the creamed combination mixing thoroughly. Blend in dates and nuts. Drop by tablespoon on ungreased cookie sheets. Bake at 350° for 15 to 18 minutes or until centers are done and edges are lightly browned. Cool on wire racks. Store in airtight containers.

TRAIL SNACK

1 pound pumpkin seeds
1 tablespoon Worcestershire sauce
2 tablespoons melted butter
2 tablespoons grated Parmesan cheese
salt

Combine all ingredients and spread out on a cookie sheet or in a jelly-roll type of pan. Toast in 350° oven stirring frequently or until the pumpkin seeds are lightly toasted. If fresh pumpkin seeds are available, toast them *un*washed as above until golden.

CAMPFIRE RACLETTE

Wrap in foil a 1- to 1-1/2-pound piece of raclette cheese (available in some delicatessens) or any other mellow-flavored cheese that melts smoothly —Monterey Jack, Fontina, Gruyère, Samsoe or regular Swiss. At dinnertime or even breakfast, place the hunk of cheese in a shallow pan close to the fire. As the cheese melts, spread it on bread or Mexican tortillas.

TRAIL LOGS

1 cup walnuts
1/2 cup cashews
1/2 cup dried apples
1 cup seedless raisins
3/4 cup pitted dates
1 teaspoon lemon juice
1-1/2 to 2 tablespoons dark Meyers rum
powdered sugar

Combine nuts and fruit and run through the finest blade of a food chopper. Mix thoroughly. Blend in the lemon juice and rum. Scooping off a heaping tablespoon of the mixture, roll into small logs about 2 by 3/4 inches. Roll in powdered sugar and allow to dry uncovered for two days or more. Store in an airtight container. Wrap tightly in foil or plastic for packing along the trail.
Makes 2-1/2 dozen rolls

WILDERNESS DESSERT OR SNACK

1/2 cup honey
1/2 cup finely chopped toasted almonds
1/4 cup finely minced candied citron
1/2 cup finely chopped walnuts
1 pound pitted dates
powdered sugar

In a bowl combine the honey, almonds, citron and walnuts. Stuff this combination into pitted dates. Roll in powdered sugar. Store in airtight container. Wrap in foil to pack.

COUNTRY CAKE

1/2 pound seedless raisins
1/2 pound pitted dates
1/2 pound dried apricots
1/2 pound dried apples
1/2 pound walnuts
1/2 pound almonds
1/3 cup orange juice

Run nuts and fruit through the finest blade of a food chopper. Blend in orange juice. Firmly press into a greased or oiled 8x4-1/2-inch loaf pan. Cover pan tightly with foil and keep at room temperature for 2 to 3 days. Remove from pan and wrap tightly in foil. Slice very thin to serve.
Makes a 3-pound loaf

HOT CHOCOLATE POWDER FOR BACKPACKERS

1 pound whole- or skim-milk powder
1 pound fine granulated sugar (not
  the type intended for icing)
1/4 pound finely ground
  bitter chocolate (not cocoa)

Combine all ingredients in a large mixing bowl. Store in an airtight container. Divide into individual packages or as desired for traveling. To prepare put 2 tablespoons in each cup, then add boiling water.

BACKPACKERS' SPICE PACKETS

(To season rice, soups, meats, eggs, etc.)

3 teaspoons dried onion (or more if desired)
3/4 teaspoon crushed dried hot red pepper
  (or amount desired)
1/8 teaspoon black pepper
1/2 teaspoon turmeric
1 teaspoon coriander
1/4 teaspoon garlic powder
2 teaspoons minced, candied ginger (optional)
1/3 cup sesame seeds

Combine ingredients and divide into individual packets. Use as a spicy seasoning for food.

Ship and Shore

Cabin, Camper and Galley Fare

I saw a ship a-sailing
A-sailing on the sea
And oh, it was all laden
With pretty things for thee.
—Nursery rhyme, c. 1750

GALLEY, CABIN AND CAMPER

The portable meal for ship and shore requires organization, daily menus and a complete food list for the exact length of your stay. Careful planning assures a favorable outcome. Since this will be a vacation, the recipes in this section call for the minimum cooking time and working effort. In addition, keep in mind the convenient ideas and recipes from the previous chapters and check the following list of basics for stocking your temporary kitchen.

Because the compact cabin, camper or galley can usually accommodate only one chef, your space and equipment is limited. But, believe it or not, you can produce many a gourmet meal from one of those kitchens.

In many cases, when out of port or in the high country (see Chapter VI Pathfinder's Knapsack), you'll have to depend upon canned goods or dehydrated foods. However, it is amazing how clever you can be when confronted with obstacles. On one vacation I found myself with two pots and two burners. After that experience I simply relied on the ideas shared in Chapter IV and restricted the main dish to a one-skillet production. The majority of these recipes are quick ideas to be enjoyed with a salad or vegetable, bread and dessert. They will be helpful wherever you are.

BASIC EQUIPMENT FOR THE GALLEY, CABIN, CAMPER

1-quart saucepan, with cover
1 frying pan or skillet (12-inch)
1 coffee pot
1 10-inch pie plate (can be used for baking other things)
3-piece set of mixing bowls
large colander
1 strainer
2-quart enameled or cast-iron casserole that can be used on range or in oven
1 large knife
1 paring knife
1 long-handled spoon
1 slotted spoon
chopping board
wire whisk or rotary eggbeater
4-sided grater with varying slots
corkscrew
can opener
Optionals
blender (time saver)
1 small square baking 8- or 9-inch all-purpose pan

CULINARY BASICS FOR CABIN, GALLEY OR CAMPER

Bacon: canned Danish or fresh
Baking soda
Baking powder
Beans: canned baked, kidney, garbanzo, etc.
Beef stock: canned or bouillon cubes
Breads: homemade, white, wheat, French (keep a few extra loaves frozen)
Butter
Cereal: breakfast, oatmeal, cornmeal
Cheese: cheddar, Monterey Jack, Swiss, Parmesan, Mozzarella, cream cheese
Chicken stock: canned or bouillon cubes
Cocoa: chocolate, semisweet and unsweetened
Coconut
Coffee: fresh ground, instant
Condiments: catsup, chili sauce, Dijon-style mustard, Worcestershire sauce, pickle relish
Cookies
Crackers: variety
Cream: dry and canned
Eggs
Fish: canned tuna, salmon, crab, shrimp, oysters, clams, sardines
Flavorings: vanilla extract, lemon, almond, orange
Flour: regular, unbleached white, cake
Freeze dried: chives and green pepper
Fruit: canned and dry: raisins, prunes, figs, apricots
Garlic: fresh, powdered
Herbs
Honey
Jams and jellies
Juice: canned or frozen
Lemons: fresh
Mayonnaise
Meat: canned tongue, ham, corned beef hash, chipped beef
Milk: canned evaporated, powdered skim
Mushrooms: dried, powdered, canned
Nuts: sunflower seeds, sesame seeds, cashews
Oil: corn oil, peanut oil, olive oil
Olives: sliced, chopped, pimiento-stuffed
Onions: fresh, dried and powdered
Pasta: assortment of dry and frozen
Pepper: black ground pepper, green pepper (dehydrated) and white pepper
Pickles: relishes
Pimientos: jar or canned
Rice: regular, brown, wild
Salt: plain, iodized, onion, garlic or seasoned
Soups: variety, canned and dry-packaged
Syrups: maple, corn and molasses
Sugar: lumps, granulated, powdered and brown (small packets)
Tea: herb, spice
Tomatoes: canned whole, paste, sauce
Vegetables: canned and always some fresh
Vinegars: cider, wine vinegar (red and white)
Wines: red, white, sherry, port (for drinking and cooking)

GALLEY, CABIN AND CAMPER SOUPS

Pity the person who has not discovered soup, for it nourishes the soul as well as the body. On long, cold and rainy winter days there is always an urge to make a steaming pot of soup. Without the inspiration, time or space, we turn to our trusty can opener and several brands of canned soups. With the aid of wines, herbs or garnishes canned and packaged soups become lively brews.

ANIMATED CANNED SOUPS

Tomato or Pea Soup: Add dash allspice, sherry or grated orange rind
Bouillon, Vegetable or Cream of Potato: Add a pinch basil or tarragon
Oyster or Clam Chowder: Add dash cayenne or Tabasco, pinch marjoram, mace or a hint of cloves
Borsch, Split Pea, Cream of Potato: Add dash cloves
Bean Soups: Add hint of ginger and sherry wine or curry
Chicken, Pea, Vegetable or Cream of Spinach: Add rosemary, nutmeg
Consommé or Cream Soups: Add bit of sage, sherry or lemon juice
Gumbo and Chowders: Add bit of chili powder, white wine
Fish Chowders: Add saffron, sherry
Vegetable Soups and Gumbos: Add a bit of chili powder, red wine

WATERCRESS SOUP

1 bunch watercress
3-1/2 to 4 cups rich chicken broth
1/2 to 1 cup white wine
1 tablespoon lemon juice

Wash and drain the watercress; remove the tough stems. Place the watercress and 1 cup of stock in the blender. Whirl until smooth. Combine with the rest of the ingredients, except the lemon juice. Heat in a saucepan. Stir in the lemon juice and serve immediately.
Serves 4

MUSHROOM CONSOMMÉ

1/2 pound fresh mushrooms
1/3 cup sherry or port wine
4 cups rich consommé
sour cream and chives

Wash, dry and dice the mushrooms and stir them into hot consommé. Turn down the heat; add the wine. Simmer 15 to 20 minutes. Top each serving with a dollop of sour cream and chives.
Serves 4

GERMAN BEER BISQUE

1 10-1/2-ounce can condensed cream of potato soup
1 10-1/2-ounce can condensed tomato or tomato bisque
1-1/2 cups beer
1 cup water

Combine above ingredients in a saucepan and bring to boiling point. Lower heat and simmer 10 to 15 minutes. Serve with pumpernickel bread or melted cheese sandwiches.
Serves 4

COLD CHILI SOUP

1 to 2 tablespoons minced onion
1/4 cup sherry wine
1 teaspoon prepared horseradish
1/2 teaspoon salt
1/2 teaspoon chili powder
1 10-1/2-ounce can tomato soup
1 cup cold water
1/2 pint sour cream
1/2 cup finely minced green pepper for garnish

Combine all the ingredients except the green pepper in the blender. Whirl until smooth. Chill 3 to 4 hours before serving. Garnish with minced green pepper. Serve with avocado spread on French bread.
Serves 4

COLD AVOCADO SOUP

1 ripe avocado
1 10-1/2-ounce can condensed consommé with gelatin
2 teaspoons lemon juice or sherry wine

Chill the consommé in the can. Cut the avocado in half. Peel and remove the pit. Cut into cubes and drop into the blender. Whirl the avocado cubes with lemon juice or sherry until smooth. Add the chilled soup. Whirl once again. Serve immediately in chilled mugs.
Variation: Add 1 can chilled vichyssoise in place of consommé and 1/2 cup sour cream. Blend until smooth. Garnish with chives.
Serves 4

INSTANT BORSCH

1 1-pound jar red cabbage
1 1-pound can shoestring beets, plus liquid
1 15-ounce can condensed beef broth
pinch crushed thyme
3 tablespoons red wine vinegar or lemon juice
4 tablespoons brown sugar

In a large saucepan combine all ingredients and bring to a gentle boil. Turn down and simmer *just* 5 to 10 minutes. Serve immediately.
Serves 4 to 6

Who riseth from a feast
With that keen appetite that he sits down?
—Shakespeare: The Merchant of Venice, 1597

OYSTER LOAF

1 loaf sourdough French bread
melted butter
2 dozen small oysters
2 eggs, beaten with 2 tablespoons water
cracker crumbs
salt and pepper
paprika
Worcestershire sauce
2 to 3 lemons

Cut the French bread in half lengthwise. Scoop out the center and discard (or save for other use, i.e. bread crumbs). Brush cut surface with melted butter. Place on a cookie sheet and toast lightly in a 425° oven. While the bread is heating, dip drained oysters in beaten eggs, then roll in cracker crumbs to coat evenly. In a preheated skillet melt 3 to 4 tablespoons butter. When hot, toss in the oysters and quickly sauté no longer than 2 to 3 minutes or just until the oysters' edges begin to curl. Spoon into one-half of the toasted loaf; sprinkle with salt, ground pepper, paprika and a bit of Worcestershire. Cover with the other half of the loaf. Eat and enjoy while hot. Pass the lemon wedges.
Serves 4 to 6

OYSTER CLUB SANDWICH

8 slices broiled bacon
8 slices tomato

To the preceding recipe for oyster loaf, add the broiled bacon strips and sliced tomato just before seasoning and topping with upper crust.
Serves 4 to 6

KÄSEBROTCHEN
(German Cheese Toast)

6 slices homemade bread
butter
2 tablespoons Dijon-style mustard
1/3 cup beer
1 cup grated cheddar cheese

Toast and butter the slices of bread. Place them in a square baking dish, but do not allow them to overlap. Blend the mustard with the beer and the cheese. Spread evenly over the toast. Place under the broiler and heat until the cheese has melted and is bubbly. Nice with sliced tomatoes, asparagus or broccoli.
Serves 4 to 6

PROVENÇAL LOAF, PISSALADIÈRE

2 large onions, chopped
butter and olive oil
1 8-ounce can tomato sauce
1/4 teaspoon crushed rosemary
   or Italian seasoning
dash garlic powder
1/2 teaspoon sugar
1 loaf French bread
sliced ripe olives
anchovy filets
grated Parmesan cheese

Sauté the chopped onions in a small amount of oil and butter. Blend in the tomato sauce and seasonings. Simmer until a thick consistency, like tomato paste.

Slice the loaf of bread in half lengthwise. Spread lightly with butter or brush with olive oil. Brown lightly under the broiler. Smear with the tomato paste; garnish with olives and a crisscross pattern of the anchovy filets as you would a pizza. Dust with Parmesan cheese. Bake at 425° for 10 to 15 minutes.
Serves 4 to 6

ENSEÑADA STUFFED ROLLS

4 crusty French rolls
2 tablespoons softened butter
2 tablespoons chopped, canned green chilies
2 green onions, chopped
1/4 cup chopped ripe olives
2 tablespoons minced green pepper
1 cup shredded cheddar cheese
1/3 cup mayonnaise
1/4 teaspoon salt
pinch garlic powder (optional)

Slice rolls in half lengthwise and scoop out most of the center. Combine and blend the rest of the ingredients in a bowl. Fill the rolls and replace the top crust. Wrap each one in foil. This much can be done ahead and refrigerated 2 to 3 hours. Remove at least 45 minutes before heating. Place rolls on a baking sheet and bake at 350° 35 to 40 minutes.
Campers: Can take these along cold and heat in foil among the coals.
Serves 4

HOT CURRIED CHEESE AND OLIVE SPECIAL

1 small can chopped ripe olives
1 small white onion, chopped
2 cups shredded, extra-sharp cheddar cheese
1/2 to 3/4 cup mayonnaise
1/2 to 1 teaspoon curry powder
English muffins

Combine ingredients thoroughly. Lightly toast split English muffins. Spread with topping and place under a preheated broiler at least 4 inches away, until bubbly and golden. This same topping can be spread on a prepared partially baked pizza dough (page 45). Bake in a 450° oven for 10 minutes, then run under preheated broiler if desired. This recipe can also be used as a hot hors d'oeuvre.
Serves 6

JOSEFINAS

1 small can peeled, roasted, green chilies
3 to 4 crusty French rolls
1/4 pound softened butter
1/8 teaspoon garlic powder
1/4 cup chopped olives
1/2 cup mayonnaise
1-1/2 cups grated cheddar cheese

Rinse "hot" seeds off the green chilies and use amount of chilies desired. Split and toast the French rolls. Blend soft butter with chilies, garlic powder, chopped olives and spread on the toasted bread. Blend the mayonnaise with the grated cheese. Spread this over the top of the chili mixture all the way to the edges. Broil approximately 7 inches from the heat until puffed and golden. Serve with Cold Avocado Soup (page 157).
Serves 3 to 4

PIZZA RAPIDO

1 recipe pizza dough (page 45)
Seasoned tomato-wine sauce (below)
anchovies
chopped salami
minced onions
chopped or sliced olives
grated cheese: Bel Paese, Mozzarella or
Provolone

Spread the prepared pizza crust with a light amount of olive oil. Then top with tomato-wine sauce, anchovies, salami, onions, olives and cheese. Bake at 450° for 10 to 15 minutes or until crust is crisp and topping is hot and bubbly. Serve immediately.
Serves 4 to 6

SEASONED TOMATO-WINE SAUCE

2 large onions, chopped
butter and olive oil
1 8-ounce can tomato sauce
1/2 teaspoon crushed Italian seasoning*
2 cloves garlic, finely minced
1 teaspoon sugar
1/4 to 1/2 cup red wine

Sauté the chopped onions in melted butter and olive oil until limp and just transparent. Stir in the tomato sauce, seasonings, garlic and sugar. Add 1/4 cup of wine to start, then simmer to make a thick consistency, adding more wine only if necessary.

**Italian seasoning:* combination of basil leaves, oregano leaves, marjoram leaves and thyme leaves.

POACHED EGGS À LA KING

6 tablespoons butter
2 tablespoons chopped onion
1 cup sliced fresh mushrooms
4 tablespoons flour
dash nutmeg
1-1/2 cups milk
1/2 cup sherry wine
1-1/2 to 2 cups diced cooked chicken
2 tablespoons diced pimiento
salt and pepper to taste
6 eggs
3 split English muffins

Melt 3 tablespoons of the butter and sauté the onion and mushrooms. Add the other 3 tablespoons of butter and blend in the flour and nutmeg. Slowly add the milk and sherry, cooking until smooth and creamy. Add the chicken, pimiento, salt and pepper. Keep on low heat. Poach the eggs and place each one on a toasted split muffin. Top each serving with the creamed chicken.
Serves 6

The world is a country which nobody ever yet
knew by description; one must
travel through it one's self
to be acquainted with it.
—Lord Chesterfield, 1747

UOVA FRITTE ALLA FONTINA

Slice Italian or French bread into 1-inch slices. Spread each slice lightly with softened butter or olive oil. Fry the bread in a skillet until golden tan and crisp. Arrange fried bread on a baking sheet and top each piece with thin slices of Fontina cheese (mild semi-soft Italian cheese). Slip into a 350° oven and heat until the cheese has melted. Serve topped with fried or poached eggs.

HUEVOS CON HONGOS
(Eggs with Mushrooms)

4 tablespoons butter
1/2 cup sliced, fresh mushrooms
1 medium onion, chopped
2 tablespoons dry sherry
6 eggs
3/4 cup milk
dash of Tabasco to taste
salt
1/4 teaspoon crushed oregano or cumin

In a skillet heat the butter and sauté the sliced mushrooms. Add the chopped onion and sauté a few minutes longer. Stir in the sherry. Simmer 10 minutes. Beat the eggs with the milk and seasonings. Stir eggs into the onion-mushroom mixture and cook as you would for scrambled eggs, keeping eggs soft and creamy. Do not overcook.
Serves 4

BASQUE OMELETTE, PIPÉRADE

1/4 to 1/2 cup minced ham
1 medium onion, chopped
olive oil and butter
1/2 cup chopped green pepper
salt and pepper
1 clove garlic, finely minced
2 tomatoes, peeled, seeded and diced
6 to 7 eggs, beaten
sprig parsley, chopped
1/4 cup shredded mild cheese, Swiss
  or Monterey Jack

In a preheated skillet sauté the ham and onion in a thin layer of oil and melted butter. Add green pepper, seasonings and chopped tomatoes. Cover and cook until vegetables are tender. Uncover and allow the tomato juices to evaporate. Pour in the beaten eggs; stir and shift the vegetables around to allow the egg to mix down and through. Sprinkle on the parsley and cheese. Reduce heat and cover. Cook just long enough for the eggs to set. Slip omelette out onto serving dish.
For Picnics: Cover serving dish with foil; wrap in several thicknesses of newspaper. This will stay warm for several hours and is also delicious served cold. Either way it's too good to leave home.
Serves 6

ZUCCHINI FRITTATA

2 tablespoons olive oil
1 medium onion, chopped
1 clove garlic, minced
6 to 7 medium zucchinis, sliced
1 large tomato, peeled and chopped
salt and pepper to taste
1 teaspoon each oregano, thyme, basil
5 to 6 eggs, beaten

In a skillet heat a thin layer of olive oil and sauté the onions and garlic. Add the zucchini and sauté another 5 to 10 minutes. Add chopped tomato and the seasonings. Cook until vegetables are tender but not mushy; they must still retain their shape. Pour on the beaten eggs, shifting the vegetables with a rubber spatula to allow the egg to run down in between. Stir gently a few times. Cover and cook over low heat until the eggs are set and begin to pull away from the sides. If the middle puffs up, prick it with a knife. When the frittata is set and nicely browned on the bottom, slide it out or invert onto a platter. Serve cut into pie-shaped wedges.
For Picnics: This dish will stay warm for several hours when traveling a short distance, if wrapped in foil and several thicknesses of newspaper. Also good cold.
Serves 6

POTATO FRITTATA

3 to 4 slices bacon, diced
1 small onion, chopped
1 pound potatoes, peeled and sliced
3 tablespoons olive oil
6 to 7 eggs, beaten
pinch chili powder
1/2 teaspoon salt
3 tablespoons grated Parmesan cheese
coarse ground black pepper

In a skillet fry the diced bacon until crisp; set aside. Toss the onions in with the bacon grease and sauté. Add potatoes to sautéed onions; cover and cook, stirring occasionally, 15 to 20 minutes. Add the olive oil if the potatoes and onions appear to be sticking. In a separate bowl beat the eggs with the chili powder, salt and Parmesan cheese. Add a bit of ground pepper to taste. Pour beaten eggs over the sautéed potatoes and add the bacon. Shift and stir ingredients around to allow the egg to mix down through the potatoes. Reduce heat, cover and cook only until the eggs are set. Slide out onto serving platter. (If desired, run the pan under the broiler to brown the top.)
Serves 4 to 5

SAN FRANCISCO'S SPECIAL

1 package, frozen, chopped spinach, defrosted and well drained
1 clove garlic, very finely minced
1 medium onion, chopped
olive oil
1-1/2 pounds lean ground beef
1/2 teaspoon crushed oregano
dash nutmeg
salt and pepper to taste
1/2 pound mushrooms, sliced
4 to 5 eggs, beaten

Defrost the chopped spinach. Drain thoroughly, squeeze out all excess moisture; set aside. Sauté the garlic and onion in a very small amount of olive oil. Add the ground beef and cook until crumbly. Add seasonings and spinach. Mix thoroughly and cook approximately 8 to 10 minutes. Sauté the mushrooms separately in 1 tablespoon of olive oil; add to the meat and spinach mixture. Add beaten eggs and work rapidly, stirring until the eggs are just set and the entire mixture is well blended. Serve immediately. Do not overcook.
Serves 4 to 6

HUEVOS DE RIO GRANDE

1 medium onion, chopped
1 clove garlic, crushed and chopped
olive oil
2 teaspoons chili powder
1 8-ounce can tomato sauce
1 cup water
1 tablespoon green pepper flakes
1 4-ounce can seeded green chilies
1/2 pound Monterey Jack cheese
1/3 cup mayonnaise
1/4 cup milk
8 eggs

Sauté chopped onion and garlic in small amount of olive oil. Blend in the chili powder. Add tomato sauce and water. Stir in green pepper flakes and simmer 20 minutes. Drain green chilies and rinse off seeds. Wrap each chili (or cut in half) around a small cube of Monterey Jack cheese. Set aside. In a bowl combine mayonnaise and milk. Break in the eggs and whip until thoroughly blended. Pour eggs into a separate, preheated skillet. Cook eggs slowly to soft scrambled-egg stage; now tuck the cheese-stuffed chilies into the eggs. Quickly transfer the pan to a 350° oven and bake until eggs set and the cheese melts. Takes approximately 10 to 15 minutes. Serve with seasoned tomato sauce (page 163).
Serves 6 to 8

ITALIAN POLENTA WITH SPINACH

1 pound fresh spinach
dash garlic powder
juice of 1/2 lemon
pinch of nutmeg
2 tablespoons olive oil
2 cups cold milk
1/2 cup yellow cornmeal
salt and pepper
1 egg
1/2 cup minced onion
1/4 cup Parmesan cheese
4 tablespoons melted butter
Seasoned tomato sauce (page 163) (optional)

Cook the spinach and drain well. Season with garlic, lemon juice, nutmeg and olive oil. Spread in a well-buttered 1-1/2-quart shallow casserole.

In a saucepan combine the cold milk and cornmeal. Cook over moderate low heat until thick and bubbly. Stir in salt and pepper to taste. Take off the heat and beat in the egg, onion and Parmesan cheese. Spread carefully over the seasoned spinach. Should be approximately 1-1/2 inches thick. Brush with melted butter; top with additional cheese. Bake at 350° for 20 minutes or until lightly browned and hot. Serve with sausages or bacon and tomato sauce.
Serves 4

MOCK MOUSSAKA

1 medium onion, chopped
1 pound ground beef or lamb
olive oil
2 cups diced, peeled tomatoes
1 small eggplant, peeled and cubed
1 clove garlic, finely minced
3 tablespoons chopped parsley
1/8 teaspoon cinnamon
1/2 teaspoon oregano
1/4 teaspoon rosemary
6 medium mushrooms, sliced
1 cup tomato juice

In a preheated skillet brown the onions and meat in a thin layer of olive oil. Pour off excess grease. Cook a few minutes to reduce the moisture. Add diced tomatoes, eggplant, seasonings and mushrooms. Blend in the tomato juice. Simmer uncovered, stirring often and reducing liquids to a saucelike consistency. Add more tomato juice if necessary to maintain a medium thickness and to prevent sticking. Serve with rice.
Serves 4

Let the heavens rejoice, and let the earth be glad;
let the sea roar, and the fulness thereof.
Let the field be joyful, and all that is therein:
then shall all the trees of the wood rejoice
—Psalm 96: 11, 12

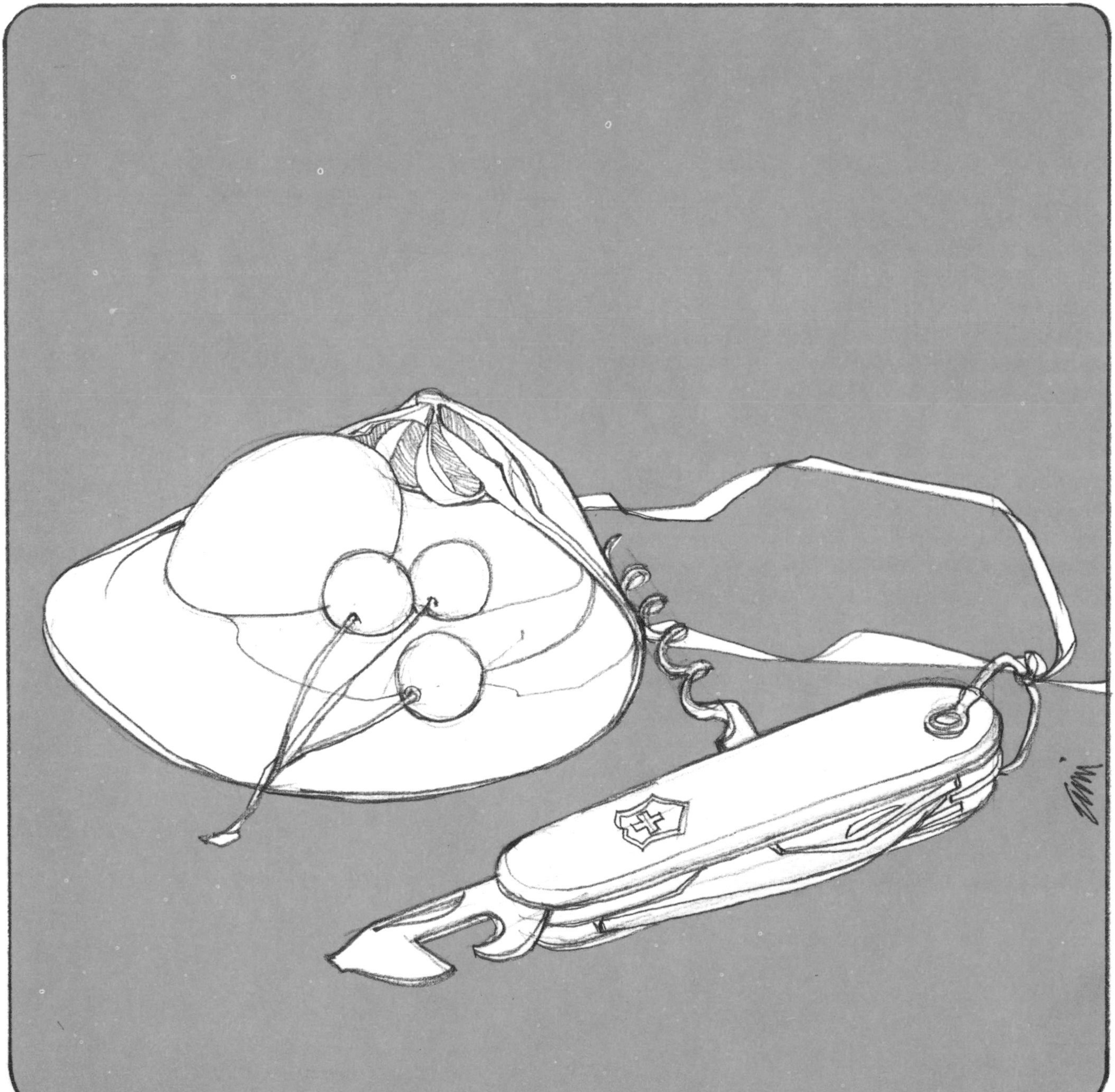

MUSHROOMS À LA CRÈME

1 pound fresh mushrooms
2 tablespoons butter
3 tablespoons dry sherry wine
1 cup sour cream, room temperature
1/2 cup grated Monterey Jack or Swiss cheese
salt and pepper to taste
English muffins

Wash, drain and dry mushrooms. Remove stems level with the caps. Mince the stems very fine; slice the caps 1/8 inch thick. Sauté both stems and caps in melted butter. Pour in the sherry and allow to simmer for several minutes. Stir in the sour cream, blending in thoroughly and adding the cheese at the same time. Just heat at this point; do not allow to boil. Serve on toasted split English muffins or regular toast points or white and/or wild rice.
Serves 4 to 6

CHICKEN LIVERS WITH WINE AND MUSHROOMS

2 tablespoons each olive oil and butter
1-1/2 to 2 pounds chicken livers, cut in half
1/4 pound fresh mushrooms, quartered
1 tablespoon chopped green pepper
2 green onions, chopped
1 tablespoon flour
1 cup dry white wine
2 tablespoons tomato catsup
1/2 teaspoon soy sauce
salt and pepper to taste
chopped parsley

Heat oil and butter in a skillet. Sauté livers and mushrooms together; then add the green pepper and onions. Sprinkle on the flour. Stir to coat well. Slowly add the wine and blend in the catsup, soy sauce, salt and pepper. Simmer for 10 minutes. Serve immediately over rice. Garnish with chopped parsley.
Serves 6

PICADILLO

1 cup raisins
1 cup port wine
2 tablespoons olive oil
1-1/2 pounds lean ground beef
1 medium onion, chopped
2 cloves garlic, minced
salt and pepper to taste
1/4 teaspoon oregano
1 teaspoon aromatic bitters (optional)
1/4 cup chopped green pepper
1 tablespoon drained capers
12 ripe olives, sliced

First place raisins in a container with the port to plump them; set aside. Heat the skillet, add the oil and brown the meat. Add the onions and garlic; sauté for a few minutes longer. Add the raisins and port to skillet. Blend in the salt, pepper, oregano and bitters. Simmer 15 to 20 minutes. Add the green pepper, capers and olives; heat another 5 minutes. Serve immediately over rice.
Serves 4 to 6

GERMAN SKILLET SUPPER

4 bockwurst or similar sausages
2 tablespoons butter
1 medium onion, sliced thin
3 strips bacon, diced
1/2 small head of cabbage, shredded
1/4 teaspoon sugar
1/2 teaspoon salt
pepper to taste
1 teaspoon caraway seeds
1/4 teaspoon allspice
1/4 cup white wine (optional)

Pierce each sausage with fork tines to prevent splitting. Melt butter in a skillet and brown onions and diced bacon. Add the shredded cabbage, seasonings and wine. Simmer 30 minutes, stirring frequently. Place sausages on top of the seasoned cabbage; cover and steam for 8 minutes.
Serves 4

KEDGEREE

1 16-ounce can salmon
1/4 to 1/2 teaspoon curry powder
2-1/2 tablespoons butter
2-1/2 tablespoons flour
1-1/2 cups milk
dash nutmeg and onion powder
speck cayenne pepper
4 hard-boiled eggs, shredded
1 cup cooked peas
1/4 cup minced pimiento
chopped parsley

Flake salmon into a bowl, removing bits of bone and skin. In a skillet mix curry powder with the melted butter, adding flour and stirring until well blended and smooth. Add milk, nutmeg, onion powder and cayenne pepper. Cook until smooth and creamy. Add flaked salmon, shredded egg, peas, pimiento and heat 3 to 5 minutes. Serve over rice. Garnish with chopped parsley.
Serves 4 to 6

CROSS-COUNTRY CHICKEN

butter and olive oil
2 large chickens, cut up
2 medium onions, chopped
2 cloves garlic, finely minced
2 teaspoons paprika
1-1/2 teaspoons salt
pepper to taste
1/2 teaspoon sugar
1/2 cup dry sherry wine
1/2 cup tomato juice
2 large tomatoes, peeled and diced
chopped parsley

In a preheated skillet, heat a thin layer of butter and olive oil. Fry the cut-up chicken. Remove and set aside as the pieces are browned. Add the onions and garlic to the pan drippings and sauté lightly. Stir and blend in the paprika, salt, pepper, sugar, sherry, tomato juice and diced tomatoes. Return chicken pieces to the sauce. Cook uncovered for 35 to 40 minutes, basting chicken pieces often with the sauce. Garnish with chopped parsley.
Serves 6

CRAB CASSEROLE

3 tablespoons chopped onion
2 tablespoons butter
2 tablespoons flour
1-1/2 cups milk
salt and pepper
pinch cayenne or dash Tabasco
1 7-ounce can crab meat, flaked
6 slices buttered toast
2 teaspoons lemon juice
2 teaspoons freeze-dried chives
2 egg whites, beaten stiff
1/2 cup mayonnaise
1/2 teaspoon Dijon-style mustard

Sauté the chopped onion in butter. Sprinkle on the flour and sauté a few minutes more. Slowly blend in the milk and seasonings. Add the flaked crab meat. Keep warm on low heat. Lay buttered toast in a 9x13-inch shallow baking dish. Take the crab mixture off the heat and blend in the lemon juice and chives. Spoon carefully over the toast. Beat the egg whites stiff until they peak. Fold in the mayonnaise and mustard. Carefully spread this over the crab mixture. Place under the broiler 7 inches from the heating unit and watch closely; it only takes a few minutes to become puffed and golden.
Variations: Salmon or tuna may be substituted for the crab meat.
Serves 6

VAGABOND STEW

oil and butter
2 pounds sirloin, sliced thin
flour
1 medium onion, chopped
1/2 teaspoon nutmeg
2 tablespoons tomato catsup
salt and pepper to taste
1 cup rich beef stock
1/4 pound fresh mushrooms, sliced
2 to 3 tablespoons drained capers

In a skillet heat a thin layer of oil and butter. Dust sliced sirloin lightly with flour, shake off excess and brown in butter and oil. Add onions and sauté until just lightly brown. Blend in the nutmeg, catsup, salt, pepper, beef stock and sliced mushrooms. Reduce heat; cover and simmer 35 minutes or until meat is tender. Blend 1 tablespoon flour with some additional beef stock and thicken the gravy. Just before serving add the drained capers.
Serves 4 to 6

Small cheer and great welcome makes a merry feast.
—Shakespeare: The Comedy of Errors, 1593

MBJ

FARINACEOUS FOODS: RICE, PASTA, POTATOES AND QUICK BREADS

What are farinaceous foods? They are any type of food containing, consisting of or made of flour, meal or starch. A meal of this type literally sticks to your ribs. Potatoes are actually a vegetable, but since they are also a starch I have placed them with the other farinaceous foods.

Although many people avoid these foods, thinking they are merely fattening, they play an important part in a balanced diet. The body needs starch which it converts into sugar to maintain basic energy levels. Without it, the body must rely on stored fat reserves for proper functioning.

PAUPER'S PILAFF

1 tablespoon butter or vegetable oil
1 medium onion, chopped
1-1/2 cups long-grain rice
3 cups water or stock
1 tablespoon dry parsley flakes
1/2 teaspoon salt
dash pepper

In a skillet, melt butter or oil and sauté the onions until they are nut brown. Add the dry rice and sauté it until tan to light nut brown. Add water or stock, sprinkle on seasonings. Cover, reduce heat and simmer on low for 35 to 45 minutes or until dry and fluffy.
Serves 4 to 6

RISO ALLA FLORENTINA

2 tablespoons olive oil
1/2 cup chopped onion
1 cup long-grain rice
2 cups rich chicken stock
1/2 cup chopped parsley
1 10-ounce package frozen chopped spinach
  or 1 pound fresh spinach, chopped
4 tablespoons olive oil
dash garlic powder
pinch salt and nutmeg
1/2 pint sour cream, room temperature

Heat skillet with 2 tablespoons olive oil. Sauté chopped onion. Add rice and stir to coat well; cook a few minutes more then add stock and chopped parsley. Cover. Reduce heat and simmer for 20 to 25 minutes or until the rice is dry and fluffy. Meanwhile cook the spinach and drain well. Toss with olive oil, garlic, seasonings and blend in sour cream. Fold into cooked rice and serve immediately.
Serves 4 to 6

HOT SPANISH RICE

2 tablespoons olive oil
1 cup long-grain rice
1/2 teaspoon sugar
1 tablespoon chili powder
2 cups water

Heat skillet with olive oil. Sauté the rice until rich nut brown. Dissolve sugar and chili powder in the water. Pour over the rice, stirring to mix well. Cover. Reduce heat and cook until all moisture is absorbed. To extend recipe, use 2 cups of rice, 3 tablespoons oil, 4 cups water and the *same amount* of seasoning. It's not quite so hot and serves more people.
Serves 4

PROMPT POTATOES

1 pound spicy Italian sausage (or 2 cans Vienna sausage)
4 tablespoons butter
3 16-ounce cans sliced white potatoes (2-2/3 cup parboiled)
2 large onions, sliced thin
salt and pepper
3 to 4 eggs, beaten
2 cups milk (or half-and-half)
1 cup grated Italian cheese: Bel Paese, Mozzarella , Provolone

Slice sausage and sauté in butter. In a well-buttered, shallow baking dish layer potatoes and onions. Sprinkle each layer with salt, pepper and sautéed sausage slices. Beat eggs with milk and pour over the layered potatoes. Top with Italian cheese. Bake at 375° for 35 to 45 minutes or until golden brown. Can serve as main dish or for brunch.
Serves 4 to 6

POTATO CASSEROLE

3 medium potatoes, peeled and cut up
1/4 cup warm milk
1/2 teaspoon baking powder
3 eggs
2 tablespoons butter
1/2 teaspoon grated lemon rind

Boil potatoes until just tender, but not mushy; drain thoroughly. Whip with the warm milk, adding the baking powder and beating in the eggs one at a time. Blend in the butter and grated lemon rind. Turn into a well-greased 1-1/2-quart casserole. Bake at 350° for 35 minutes.
Serves 4

SCALLOPED POTATOES

4 potatoes, peeled and thinly sliced
1-1/2 cups grated cheddar cheese
2 green onions, finely minced
1/2 cup condensed chicken stock
butter

Combine the sliced potatoes with grated cheese and minced onions. Turn into a well-buttered casserole. Pour chicken stock over mixture. Dot with butter and top with additional grated cheese. Bake at 350° for 45 minutes, or until hot, bubbly and browned on top.
Serves 6

SPAGHETTI WITH CLAM SAUCE

2 tablespoons each olive oil and butter
2 cloves garlic, minced
1 large onion, chopped
3 medium tomatoes, peeled, seeded and diced
1/4 teaspoon salt
pepper to taste
1/2 teaspoon each thyme, oregano
1 8-ounce can tomato sauce
1 cup clam juice
dry white wine
2 10-ounce cans whole baby clams
  (or minced if preferred)
1 pound pasta, cooked, drained and
  tossed with melted butter
chopped parsley
Parmesan cheese

Heat oil and butter in a skillet. Sauté the garlic and onions. Add tomatoes, salt, pepper, seasonings, tomato sauce and clam juice. Simmer over low heat for 30 to 35 minutes, thinning sauce if necessary with a splash of wine. Turn the drained clams into the sauce and heat for 3 to 5 minutes. Serve over hot buttered spaghetti, sprinkled generously with chopped parsley and Parmesan cheese.
Serves 4 to 6

PASTA ALLA CARBONARA

1/2 pound bacon, diced
4 eggs, room temperature, beaten
5 tablespoons Parmesan and
  Romano cheese mixture
1 clove garlic, crushed
3 tablespoons chopped parsley
coarse ground pepper
1 pound rigatoni ribbed noodles
  (or pasta of your choice)

In a skillet sauté the bacon bits until crisp. Drain on paper towel. Beat eggs and add cheese, garlic, chopped parsley and ground pepper. Cook pasta in boiling salted water, drain and immediately toss with the egg mixture. Pasta must be hot to slightly cook the eggs as you toss it. Serve at once garnished with the crisp bacon bits. Can be served as a main dish with tossed salad and French bread.
Serves 4 to 6

Accuse not nature, she hath done her part;
Do thou but thine.
—John Milton: Paradise Lost, VIII, 1667

PASTA ALLA NORCIA

1 pound pasta of your choice
8 to 9 slices bacon, diced
1 medium onion, chopped
1 to 2 cloves garlic, finely minced
1/2 teaspoon crushed marjoram
grated Parmesan and Romano cheese

Cook the pasta in water and while it is boiling, sauté diced bacon and onion in a skillet until onion is brown and bacon crisp. Add minced garlic and sauté a few minutes longer. Sprinkle on the marjoram and set aside on low heat. Keep it warm while you drain pasta. Toss with cooked pasta and pass the cheese.
Serves 4

GOURMET MACARONI AND CHEESE

2 cups uncooked macaroni
2 tablespoons vegetable oil
butter
2 cups cubed cheese: cheddar, Swiss or Gruyère
dash cayenne pepper
1/4 teaspoon salt
1 to 1-1/2 teaspoons Dijon-style mustard
2 eggs, beaten
1-1/2 cups milk
1/2 cup white wine
topping: seasoned croutons or
  1/2 cup buttered, seasoned bread crumbs

Cook macaroni in boiling, salted water and oil. Do not overcook; when done rinse and drain. Butter a 2-quart casserole and combine macaroni, cubed cheese, cayenne pepper, 1/4 teaspoon salt and mustard. Beat the eggs, milk and wine together. Blend in with the macaroni and cheese mixture. Cover with topping. Bake at 350° for 40 to 50 minutes.
Serves 6

RICOTTA CHEESE PANCAKES

1 cup ricotta cheese
1 teaspoon baking powder
3 eggs
2 tablespoons melted butter
2 teaspoons sugar
1/2 cup sifted unbleached white flour
2/3 cup milk

Combine ingredients and beat until smooth or put them in a blender in order given, mixing a portion at a time until smooth. Pour mixture onto a lightly greased, preheated grill in 2-inch rounds over a medium-low heat. Turn cakes when small bubbles form on the surface. Serve hot, dusted with powdered sugar. These are lovely and light, like French crêpes and very tasty with strawberry or raspberry preserves, melted butter and maple syrup, along with bacon or sausages. They can also be used as dessert pancakes.
Serves 3 to 4

PAIN PERDU (LOST BREAD)

4 eggs
pinch salt
3 tablespoons sugar
3/4 cup milk
1/4 cup dry sherry wine
6 to 7 pieces thick sliced white bread
(or French bread)
butter
powdered sugar
cinnamon
honey

In a bowl beat together the eggs, salt and sugar. Blend in the milk and sherry thoroughly. Dip and soak each slice of bread in the liquid, turning each piece several times to be sure it is evenly saturated. Fry in butter as you would French toast. Serve hot with powdered sugar, cinnamon and honey.
Serves 4 to 6

PRAIRIE BREAD

1/2 cup chopped onions
1 tablespoon butter
1/2 cup cornmeal
1/2 cup unbleached flour
1/2 cup fine bread crumbs
4 teaspoons sugar
1 tablespoon baking powder
1 egg
3/4 cup milk

Sauté onions in butter. In a large mixing bowl, combine the dry ingredients. In another bowl beat the egg with the milk. Pour into dry ingredients all at once. Stir quickly and mix well; fold in sautéed onions. Pour into a well-greased 8-inch square baking pan. Bake at 350° for 25 to 30 minutes.
Serves 4 to 6

POPOVERS

3 eggs
1 cup milk
1/4 teaspoon salt
1 cup unbleached white flour
2 tablespoons melted butter or oil

Oil or grease muffin cups. (I prefer Teflon-lined muffin tins for popovers.) Blend eggs and milk with rotary beater or blender. Add salt, flour and melted butter or oil. Preheat the empty muffin tin for 5 minutes. Then pour batter into the muffin cups, 2/3 full. Put in oven preheated to 425°; *reduce the temperature to 375° after 10 minutes* and bake at 375° for 40 to 45 minutes.
Makes 12 popovers

CALIFORNIA CORNBREAD

2 eggs
1/2 cup sugar
1-1/2 cups sifted unbleached flour
3 teaspoons baking powder
pinch salt
1 cup cornmeal
1 cup milk
4 tablespoons melted butter

Beat the eggs and sugar together until light. In another bowl combine all the dry ingredients. Blend dry ingredients into the eggs and sugar alternately with the milk. Add the melted butter. Pour into a well-greased and floured 8-inch baking pan. Bake at 400° for 30 minutes or until center is done. Delicious for breakfast or serve hot with chili beans.
Serves 4 to 6

TOAD IN THE HOLE

12 link sausages
salt and pepper
3 eggs
1 cup milk
1 cup unbleached white flour

Parboil and then lightly broil the sausages. Place them in a shallow *well*-greased baking dish with approximately 4 tablespoons of the melted fat from the sausages. Sprinkle lightly with salt and pepper. With a rotary beater or blender combine the eggs, milk and flour until smooth. Pour batter over the prepared sausages and fat; bake at 375° for 35 to 40 minutes. Serve with eggs. Excellent for breakfast.
Serves 4 to 6

Index

Index

Index

Index

SALADS AND SALAD DRESSINGS

BEVERAGES

SOUPS

DESSERTS

DIANE DE LORME MACMILLAN

Although a fine arts major in college, Diane MacMillan turned her creative efforts to the kitchen after marriage. The encouragement of friends who continually asked for her recipes convinced her that she would like to write cookbooks. For the past five years she has worked almost full time creating, testing and writing recipes and in that time produced the manuscripts for five cookbooks of various lengths. The first to be published, "Coffee Cuisine," was brought out last year by Artists and Writers Publications, San Rafael, California. Mrs. MacMillan also has her own weekly radio show, "Kitchen Time in Marin." She is married to architect Don MacMillan and they live in San Rafael, north of San Francisco.

ERNI YOUNG

During an astoundingly prolific 20-year career Erni Young has worked simultaneously as an artist, architectural designer, planner and graphic designer. Presently he heads Erni Young NSCA and Associates, Designers, Planners and Consultants. He is also an Associate Professor in the Department of Design at the University of California, Berkeley. His fine arts commissions include sculpture and murals for numerous hospitals and other public buildings throughout California, working in a wide variety of media ranging from bas relief and leaded glass to painted tapestry.

Mr. Young was formerly associate director of Stone, Marraccini and Patterson, the San Francisco architectural and planning firm with which Diane MacMillan's husband is associated. She became an ardent admirer of his work, he of her cooking and thus the present collaboration was born.